An Angler's Guide to
SMART BAITS

An Angler's Guide to
SMART BAITS

Tips and Tactics on Fishing
Twenty-First Century Artificials

ANGELO PELUSO

Foreword by Mark Sosin

Skyhorse Publishing

This book is dedicated to all the pioneering men and women of science and technology whose wisdom and genius has elevated civilization and made the world in which we live a better place. And to those enterprising leaders of the fishing industry who have embraced that science and technology to create the smartest artificial baits ever presented to sport fish.

CONTENTS

FOREWORD

No matter how sophisticated an angler you may be, fishing will always have an element of mystery. If the mystery and the challenge weren't there, fishing would not have the appeal it does to millions of people. It doesn't matter if your preference is freshwater or salt or both, game fish seem to get more sophisticated and harder to fool with each passing year. That's because the smartest fish survive to spawn and give birth to even smarter fish.

Whether you are a casual user of artificial lures, simply thought about trying them sometime, or you're a dedicated aficionado, count on discovering that many of the old-time baits are not as effective as they once were. The newest artificials are much more realistic and boast scientific designs that trigger fish into striking them. Angelo Peluso calls these artificials smart baits and guides the reader from early designs to the most modern on the market today. He points out that the latest and most effective artificials rely on space-age synthetics, realistic designs, and applied science.

The earliest examples of artificial baits copied the size, shape, and characteristics of a fish's natural prey. As Angelo points out, all of these lures may work when fish are in an active feeding mode and ready to attack anything they can ingest. Today's smart baits try to do one more thing: They attempt to stimulate fish into attacking a lure when they are not in a feeding state. It should be noted that fish expend a great deal of energy when they are feeding and often spend hours afterward basically resting while they digest the food. Consider, too, that the colder the water, the shorter the feeding time, the longer the time to digest, the less frequently that they will feed, as well as the shorter distance and slower speed they will chase a lure.

With all the space-age artificials available for purchase, my favorite lure is still the very versatile lead-headed bucktail. If I were limited to only one lure, that would be my choice. Most anglers don't know that every saltwater survival kit in World War II contained one. Today's bucktails are dramatically better than the original deer hair models. Bucktails now have realistic heads that work better on the retrieve, laser-sharpened hooks, holographic eyes, plus natural as well as synthetic materials for tails. Add a soft plastic extended tail to the bucktail and it becomes one of the most efficient and productive artificials available.

To be successful in today's marketplace as well as on the water, smart baits must have the capacity to create the perception of live food. When you think about it, an artificial lure is simply a deceptive imposter of a fish's natural food. Fish primarily rely on smell, sound, and sight to locate and isolate a food source. A well-engineered smart bait must appeal to one or more of these senses as it moves through the water. Years ago, anglers had to impart all the action to an artificial. Now, many of the smart baits create their own action.

If a particular type of lure catches fish, it often will work in both freshwater and salt. Angelo calls these crossover lures. A well-designed plastic worm is a perfect example. I have personally caught everything on one from largemouth bass and pike to bonefish and sailfish. And, you can add them as tails on other lures. Consider, too, that soft plastics can absorb scent, which also attracts fish.

Based on the latest science as well as practical field experience, Angelo Peluso's *An Angler's Guide To Smart Baits* is not a book to be read and then put aside. It is a volume that belongs in every angler's library as an ongoing reference. If you presently fish artificial lures in freshwater or salt, or if you hope to fish them in the future, you have to read this book. I've fished in more countries than I can count for more species than I can remember, and I still learned a lot reading this book. I guarantee you will too.

—Mark Sosin

PREFACE

I have been infatuated with fish ever since I was a young boy. My uncle Tony introduced me to the hobby of keeping tropical fish. He helped set up my first tank, and from there I soon entered the realm of raising live bearers. Before long I had seven operating fish tanks in a spare room of my parents' apartment. Not having access back then to the plethora of today's electronic toys that all kids seem to now enjoy, I would sit in that room for hours and watch the fish: how they swam, how they fed, and how they interacted with their tank mates. It was fascinating to me to observe those behaviors, and that pastime further fueled my fascination with fish. My tropical fish hobby eventually developed into a yearning to catch fish, and by the age of ten I had caught my first yellow perch on a Pearl Wobbler spoon.

My dad rowed me around a small lake in upstate New York during one of our annual vacation treks to the country. I had just gotten a new-fangled spinning rod and reel, and was getting the knack of casting when the lure stopped dead and my line came alive with the throbbing of a fighting fish.

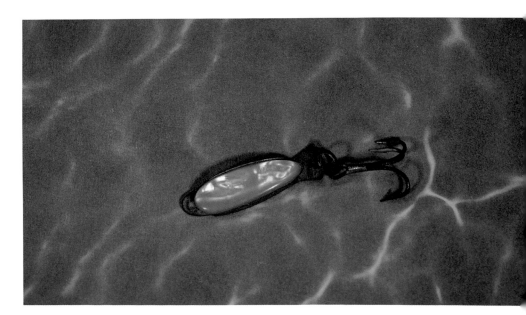

The vintage Pearl Wobbler used to catch my first fish on an artificial lure.

That catch for me was as close to fishing magic as was possible. The fact that a fish would actually eat a "make-believe" imitation of something live intrigued me more than Mickey Mantle and Roger Maris belting home runs out of the "house that Ruth built," and set in motion a quest to continue to catch fish on artificial baits.

At one point in my maturation as an angler, largemouth bass became the focus of most of my attention, and I fished for them almost exclusively. Although I enjoyed catching bass on both top-water and swimming plugs, a beneficial byproduct of bass fishing was the exposure to a seemingly endless array of artificial baits, and continual innovation of those lures. Over the years I also became somewhat proficient at catching bass on crank baits, spinner baits, suspending baits, jigs, plastic worms, and a wide assortment of soft plastic baits. The fact that each form of those artificial baits had unique applications required me to learn different techniques and retrieves. Those methods paid handsomely with other fishing endeavors, since such skills are often transferable from one species to the next, and from freshwater to saltwater. Furthermore, as bass fishing transitioned to a competitive sport, manufacturers raised the bar for lure performance by creating new adaptations to artificial lures that would give anglers novel advantages over their quarry.

While freshwater bass and trout had captivated much of my attention as a young angler, perhaps the biggest moment in my development as a saltwater angler occurred the moment I hooked and landed my first striped bass. The year was 1964, and the place was on the outskirts of the Bronx, under the City Island bridge. It amazes me that I can still completely visualize that entire event as the epiphany unfolded. I stood on a concrete abutment under the small bridge, casting a jointed Rebel Minnow on a medium-action spinning rod.

The tide was running strong and a current seam had formed well within casting distance of my position. I had made dozens of casts as dusk enveloped the area. And then one fateful cast placed the swimming lure at the edge of the seam. Two twitches of the rod tip was all it took for the bass to strike. Once landed and released that bass and the artificial I caught it on set a series of events in motion that would govern the way I would forever fish. Not too long after that first striped bass, I began fishing a cove located not far from that same bridge. This cove had a reputation among "old salts" as being a local honey hole for striped bass. A friend of mine had a car, so we took frequent trips to this spot. While our striper luck fishing this cove was far from what we had expected, the old-time regulars finally acknowledged our presence and were willing to share their knowledge of the rising and falling tides, and more importantly, the habits of local striped bass. One day fishing in that cove sealed the deal for me with artificial lures. Neither my friend nor I nor anyone else in that cove had caught or even hooked a bass. Although the resident "sharpies" had been fishing bait, they threw in the towel and talked about trying again on another day. Yet, my friend and I continued to cast. Making non-stop repetitive casts, I found myself somewhat in a zone that had become akin to a mindless routine. If I made one cast that day I must have made a thousand.

The old-time bait-fishermen just sat and watched. I heard one say: "They won't catch anything fishing like that. Times like this all the fish want is bait." I paid no attention to that unsolicited advice and kept casting. Just about the time the tide was halfway to its high point, we noticed the dimpling of bait on the surface and the dorsal fins of feeding fish. We couldn't quite

The classic Rebel Minnow that hooked my first striped bass has endured the test of time.

reach those fish but we waited. Finally, with rising water and bait movement, the fish were within our range, and then we caught striped bass one after another until our arms gave out. One of the old timers shouted over to me, "That's what it means to keep pluggin'. You guys deserve those fish." More so than the acknowledged acceptance into that cove's inner circle, the lessons of that experience convinced me that artificial baits are not only effective, but my preferred way to fish.

The allure of artificial baits opened up an entirely new world for me, so much so that to this day I rarely use any form of natural bait when fishing. Whether casting hard baits, soft baits, metal lures, or flies, today's anglers can feel confident that their baits are the embodiment of space-age synthetics, realistic designs, and applied science. Furthermore, contemporary lure designers have a thorough understanding of both game fish and prey behaviors and physiology, and anglers now enjoy some of the most sophisticated and intriguing artificial baits ever available to anglers. So please join me on a journey of discovery into the "smartest" baits ever to tempt fish to strike.

—Angelo Peluso
Long Island Sound, 2017

INTRODUCTION

Primitive man's primary goal was quite fundamental: to stay alive. Living in a world where the basic daily operating premise was to eat or be eaten, our ancient ancestors had to manipulate their environments or perish. They especially needed to gain a competitive advantage over those carnivores that would delight in dining on their two-legged neighbors. Just think where modern humankind would be if those first cave dwellers didn't engage their "flight" mechanisms and elude the saber tooth tigers that stalked them. Natural selection would surely have prevailed. But they persevered and they overcame daunting challenges. While shelter and clothing were the easier of the three basic necessities of life for the primitives to acquire, the ability to gather food was very much dependent upon instincts and a learned set of skills. Early hunters used whatever was available to incapacitate and kill prey. They learned through trial and error that sticks and stones could indeed break bones, and that smashing rocks to skulls caused a blunt force trauma that could kill their next meal. They also figured out that pointed sticks thrust into the vital organs of prey also got the job done.

With time and experience they sharpened sticks to form more lethal spears, shaped tree branches into wooden clubs, and transformed rocks into bludgeoning instruments like axes. But primeval ingenuity to more efficiently capture game would not be stifled. Concealed dug-out pits, traps, snares, and deadfall devices all complemented the hunter's simpler arsenal of sticks and stones. An atlatl, or spear-thrower, eventually evolved that enabled the hunter to utilize leverage and stored energy to hurl darts with greater efficiency and speed. Although those primitive hunters may not have been fully aware of the engineering theories behind the design of the atlatl, science nonetheless had begun to creep into their hunting techniques. Bows and arrows were next to come onto the scene. While there is some debate as to whether this occurred seventy thousand or ten thousand years ago, the bow and arrow revolutionized the process of harvesting game animals. And then sometime around the ninth century, the Chinese Tang Dynasty invented gunpowder. Firearms followed, and warfare as well as hunting changed forever.

The harvesting of land-based animals was not the only game in town for early primitives. Fish, too, were a major source of sustenance. Finfish and seafood were unquestionably on the menu of those Neanderthals and Homo sapiens living near fresh water or salt water. Evidence of fishing activities dates back more than forty thousand years. Indications of fishing exist in numerous forms: archaeological finds of remnant fish bones in primitive encampments and more permanent communities; discarded mollusk shells and shell mounds; and evidence of fish consumption via the extraction of bone collagen from the skeletal remains of early humans. It is also known that our Stone Age ancestors used fish hooks carved from animal bone. Furthermore, primitive fishermen were in some ways like their modern descendants in that they liked to document their food gathering exploits as a means to communicate a hunting and gathering lifestyle. Modern man achieves this through the use of videos, photos, books, and social media, while the Neanderthals and early humans used cave drawings and rock etchings. Since much of that "rock art" depicted mammals, birds, and fish, it is reasonable for us to conclude that animals played a major role in the lives of early man.

Anthropologists believe that the earliest of primitive "fishermen" used their hands to trap and catch fish in streams, rivers, and the shallows of ponds and lakes. While this degree of athletic prowess certainly got the job done, the amount of energy and calories expended to capture a meal was inefficient, and led to the use of various implements and tools that made the task a lot easier. At first spears utilized simple points sharpened into the wood to impale the fish. Over time, chiseled stone and eventually iron was used. Straight points evolved into barbed tips, and devices like gigs emerged with multiple pronged points designed to securely hold speared fish. Nets, fish traps, and even bows and arrows were deployed as a means to catch fish that frequented shallow water in both fresh water and salt water.

Fast forward to "modern" man. It believed that as far back as 2000 BCE, the Egyptians used simple fishing rods and line to catch fish. Other cultures like the Chinese, Japanese, Romans, and Greeks also used rod-like tools to catch fish, presumably in a sporting manner. While those fishing roots extend back thousands of years and were engaged in mostly as a means to secure food, it is generally accepted that recreational sport fishing, or angling as it came to be known, had its first true beginnings with the publication in 1496 of Dame Juliana Berners's "Treatyse of Fishing with an Angle." That essay was part of *The Book of St. Albans* and is considered the first primer on sport fishing. The treatise included information on rod building, lines, baits,

Izaac Walton's classic, *The Compleat Angler.*

artificial flies, and places to fish. Other authors wrote subsequent essays, but the next significant work of the times on the subject of angling, particularly fishing with artificial flies, was the 1653 volume of *The Compleat Angler* by Izaac Walton.

Walton's defining work generated broad interest in recreational fishing and new growth during the infancy of this emerging sport. From that point forward the world began to see innovations that embraced technologies of the times. More effective hooks and enhanced bamboo rod building techniques emerged, as did methods for the making of fishing lines. Anglers started to use reels to store lines, and line guides started to appear on rods. In addition to traditional natural baits, artificial flies became very popular throughout England and Europe. Along with the eventual colonization of North America, the English brought the traditions of recreational fly fishing with them to the new world. The "sport" took hold in the nineteenth century, endured, and blossomed. After the Industrial Revolution, manufacturers applied major advances in technology and processes to the production of fishing tackle. It was during this time that casting reels began to have a more modern resemblance, and metal, spoon-like lures and artificial wooden plugs began to gain in popularity. At first the early plugs were simple lures carved from blocks of wood with hooks attached, and fashioned in a manner that when retrieved would move about like an injured baitfish or aquatic creature. But anglers of all eras have always sought out the holy grail of lure and baits, seeking a magic of sorts that would enthrall their favorite fish species. Those simple plugs and lures soon began to take on more sophisticated design features. Metal lips caused the wooden plug lures to wiggle seductively or dive when retrieved. Jointed or articulated plugs gave more lifelike action to artificial baits to stimulate more strikes. Lure makers painted the bodies of the lures so as to create a more natural look.

Wood and metal artificial baits dominated the fishing scene until the advent of plastics. Those synthetics, along with the use of fiberglass in rod

Classic baitcasting outfit and wooden plug.

building and the introduction of the spinning reel, fundamentally revolutionized the fishing industry. The post–World War II era put a spotlight on the spinning technique and the popularity of those reels soared, along with lighter and more finessed artificial plastic bait that could then be cast with ease and efficiency. Monofilament lines, and more recently braided lines, added to the sport's advancement. Sport fishing's next big leap came as a byproduct of the space age and the materials and technologies that emerged from those achievements of flight. It is common in the current era of manufacturing to see the use of hi-tech materials like boron, titanium, exotic polymers, resins, and nanofibers in modern fishing tackle.

Recreational sport fishing has indeed come a very long way since the days of the cane pole, bobber, and earthworm. While plastic still prevails as a dominant material for hard and soft artificial baits, contemporary lures have evolved to embrace significant science into their designs. That science includes not only the engineering of artificial baits, but also to how lures more accurately mimic the baitfish they are intended to replicate, and the behaviors of fish that will hopefully eat the lures. The blending of all those elements has created the most advanced replicas of aquatic life forms and a generation of baits that are indeed "smarter" than those of previous eras. While many classic and traditional baits are as effective today as they were decades ago, today's artificial lures are the beneficiaries of advanced technology, engineering, biology, and chemistry. To understand how contemporary hard and soft baits function one needs to also understand the science behind their designs. *An Angler's Guide to Smart Baits* will lead you through the maze of contemporary soft and hard baits, as well as their design, functionality, and methods for fishing. In addition, I will address the sensory appeal of modern baits to fish in detail, and methods to maximize modern fishing baits to stimulate the sensory mechanisms of fish to yield greater hook-up ratios. The wisdom of researchers, lure designers, scientists, and lure manufacturers will also hopefully augment your understanding of new-age smart baits. Now join me on this journey of discovery that is sure to make your own fishing experiences more enjoyable and more productive.

CHAPTER 1

FISH DECOYS AND WOODEN PLUGS

Contemporary outdoor sporting traditions are well rooted in prehistoric and primitive pre-occupation with survival. Our ancient predecessors pursued fish and game for one purpose: to put food in the cave. More modern humans have embraced the spirit of the chase to include not only the nutritional value of our harvest but also the inherent sport of it all. Over the course of millennia man adapted his techniques and became ever more efficient in the process of the "hunt." Primitive spears, hooks and snares evolved into the sophisticated fishing tackle, hunting equipment, and the high-tech gear presently available to us. Within the realm of sport fishing, today's artificial baits are marvels of modern science in terms of chemistry, technology, and engineering. These fraudulent baits often move, taste, and smell better than the real thing. And some are so anatomically correct you'd be hard pressed to tell authentic from fake. But there was a time in the not-too-distant past—as recently as the early to mid-twentieth century—when modern man still used primitive wooden fish forms, dangled seductively on string, to lure fish to where they could be captured, most often with the use of a spear. Some of the more primitive forms of fish decoys, especially those used by Native Americans, predate by centuries the first wooden plugs. But in all respects these hand-crafted decoys accomplished virtually the same end goal as contemporary plugs and artificial baits: they grabbed the attention of fish and lured them into a position of vulnerability.

When we think of contemporary lures our thoughts most often revert to plugs, plastics, and tins. In their most fundamental forms, artificial lures have been the mainstay of non-bait fishing in the United States since the late 1800s as their use coincided with the manufacture and utilization of the first generation of conventional fishing tackle. Flies have been around even longer,

Native American fish decoy.

with hair, wool, and feather creations dating back to ancient Macedonia. But positioned in the middle of all this a rather unique and often-overlooked form of lure that is a close first cousin to the wooden plug: The fish decoy.

Fish decoys were used primarily by those fishing through the ice and were, therefore, most prevalent in colder regions of the United States and Canada. There is some belief that inhabitants of the coldest regions of northeast Asia also used fish decoys. Native Americans employed the most widely-practiced applications of ice spearing with the use fish decoys in regions of Canada, New York, Minnesota, Wisconsin, Michigan, and Alaska. There is some evidence that ancestors of modern Alaskan Eskimos used carved ivory fish decoys as far back as 1000 AD. New York State is acknowledged as one of the first places in North America where Native Americans used fish decoys as a means to catch fish. Those early native people left behind a rich legacy of decoy carving craftsmanship, replete with examples of carved fish effigies, bone and ivory hooks, and barbed spears. While fish decoys, like their waterfowl counterparts, evolved over time into forms of decorative folk art, the older, original designs were used principally as working decoys with the express objective of luring fish to the spear. Many of those fish decoy templates were the inspiration for early wooden plugs.

Fish decoys were the precursors to modern plugs and lures.

With the exception of the most primitive fish decoys carved from bone and ivory, early craftsmen crafted many working fish decoys from wood. These wooden lures typically resembled fish or other "critters," such as frogs, turtles, crayfish, mice, and salamanders. For the most part, the type of fish

Large carp decoys like this one were used to lure large predatory fish like pike and muskies.

form was irrelevant. It could be in the shape of a trout, small bass, perch, chub, catfish, bluegill, a small carp, or any number of other fish facsimiles. Profile, coloration, and size were the most important general features and elements of attraction. Size would vary from small decoys of but a few inches in length to massive decoys of fifty inches that anglers used as "coaxers" for spearing large fish like sturgeon. All sizes in between that range enticed fish such as bass, trout, walleye, perch, pike, whitefish, and muskies.

Fish decoys would be either painted or retained in a natural wood state. Carved or metal fins finished the detail of a decoy to render a more realistic appearance. Lure makers occasionally burned into the wood to create a natural texture or mottled effect. Native Americans would often use leather inserted into natural-wood decoys to replicate tails and fins. Some would even carve curved bodies and tails to effect a more lifelike action when manipulated on the jigging stick. As an interesting corollary, fish decoys over time evolved into more colorful renditions of the baits they were used to imitate—much like modern plugs featuring some of the most eye-catching finishes ever applied to artificial lures. Anglers believed those vibrant colors worked best in dark and dingy waters, especially for such prized fish as pike and muskies. Eventually—and with the wider availability of hooks—it didn't take much of a leap of faith for some enterprising soul to attach those hooks to decoys and move us down the path toward wooden plugs.

The purpose of the fish decoy is simple: Jiggle a submerged decoy with a short jigging stick through a hole in the ice to simulate a form of live prey,

Factory decoys were mass manufactured as an alternative to hand carved decoys.

wait for a predator fish like a pike to arrive and investigate the situation, and then spear the intruder. Technique varied and sometimes the angler extracted the decoy from the cold water to further agitate the game fish before spearing it. Often, the predator actually impaled itself on the spear as it attacked and grabbed the decoy in its jaws. The set-up is similar to what is still used today in modern ice fishing. By attaching the line at different tie-in locations one changes the orientation of how the decoy rests in water and how it behaves when jigged. For example, a nose-up, nose-down, or straight horizontal posture. Generally, the fish decoy moves slowly up and down at the terminal end of the jigging stick. This imparts action to the decoy that invites curious predators within range of the spear when they come to investigate the movement and disturbance.

Early spearing anglers constructed structures of small tree branches over the ice holes to block any external light distractions from interfering with the view of a fish as its bulk filled the hole. Within that darkened space, traditional Native American "spearers" would typically lie in a prone position searching the hole beneath. The fish decoy would be jigged in the hopes of attracting a food fish. When the unsuspecting fish would appear in the hole, the angler would thrust the spear hard and fast into the target. Anglers in the past fished from ice shacks and shanties similar to those still in use today for ice fishing. Although fishing methods and techniques have

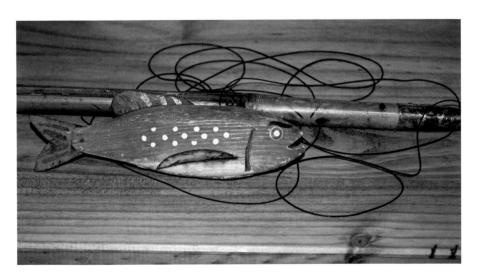

Fish decoy and jigging stick.

changed from the glory days of ice spearing to modern angling times, a fundamental concept has remained the same: fool a fish into believing your offering is authentic and you can catch it, or in the case of fish decoys, spear it.

While fish decoys had a singular purpose for ice jigging, one could propose that the way in which the decoys were carved and fished had much to do with the eventual design concept for early wooden plugs. In many instances, size, shape, and use of color follow form and function from fish decoys to plugs. There is also an interesting progression in the design process for both decoys and plugs, as well as some common parallel development paths. The most obvious of these characteristics is that ice-fishing decoys characteristically resembled specific species of fish. Very early fish decoys, such as Native American decoys, most often had just natural wood finishes. In some instances those early fishermen would add pieces of subtle material like leather to form the tail section of the decoys, providing for some enticing movement when jigging the lure. We see that kind of inherent movement built into all of today's artificial baits. As the years progressed, functional working decoys of the 1930s through the 1960s featured more vibrant colors. When fish decoys attained collectible status, many had ornate painting, and were therefore differentiated from the working fish carvings. This is much

Many of today's modern baits are designed with a high degree of anatomical accuracy.

like duck decoys that are used for the hunt, compared to those that are carved and decorated for display only. Early wooden fishing plugs, like those of the Creek Club designs, were more impressionistic in nature and intended to be fished in a manner that simulated a real bait form that was either injured or vulnerable. Those plugs were either straight and one-piece, or segmented and articulated for more action and seductive movement. Only recently have we seen contemporary plugs, both wooden and plastic, manufactured with a high degree of anatomical accuracy. This trend is quite reminiscent of peak years of fish decoy use, and a method that now occurs in many soft and hard artificial baits.

Although wooden fish decoys may be the predecessors of wooden fishing plugs to an extent, some plugs or lure-like gadgets can be traced back to primitive man. Yet, history has it that James Heddon, through an inadvertent action, was the first of modern-day anglers to recognize the value of a "plug" carved from a block of wood as a lure to attract and catch largemouth bass.

Early plugs underwent constant modifications to enhance effectiveness.

As the legend goes, Heddon discarded a piece of wood from a whittling session by throwing it into a pond. Fate intervened and a largemouth bass struck the scrap of wood. Fascinated by this event, Heddon was motivated to refine his carvings and he ultimately created the renowned and iconic Dowagiac Casting Lure. From that point on others capitalized on the success of Heddon's creation and a plug-building industry ensued. Those first-generation plugs were most often floating lures constructed of a lightweight wood like basswood or balsa. They were typically made into a one-piece lures but the first variation resulted in jointed lures by adding a second piece of carved wood to the primary section so as to simulate the swimming motion of a tail. Furthermore, early modifications included metal lips that enhanced the "wobble" factor of the plug during retrieval. Painted finishes that could mimic the tones and coloration of various prey, from baitfish to frogs and the juvenile stages of other game fish. Most early plugs were designed to target freshwater bass, pike, and salmon.

Over time, the topwater orientation of plugs expanded to include lures that would sink and shimmy below the surface of the water when retrieved. This added another measure of versatility to plugs since they could now be fished at different points in the water column where fish would feed and move about. In some cases this depth penetration was the result of weight added to the plug, and in other instances it was the design or the length and angle of a "lip" that governed the depth to which the lure would dive. Some lure makers also realized the appeal of sound for attracting fish to the plugs. Concave heads create a popping sound when retrieved, hence the birth of the "popper." In some instances lure makers inserted rattles or small metal balls into chambers of the lures to emit sound. As plastic became a more popular material for lure construction, other significant design attributions also became available. Makers could easily shape plugs into many forms and add adjuncts during the molding process, such as rattles and sound-producing chambers. As plastic lures continued to evolve, more effective and efficient suspending or neutral buoyancy baits developed from these game-changing synthetic materials. Those advancements allowed the angler to fish the lure in a manner that let it descend with minimal retrieving action. During the descent the bait could then be moved slowly, as if it was an injured or stunned baitfish attempting to regain its stability. These characteristics give an artificial lure the appearance of an easy meal, and fish respond accordingly.

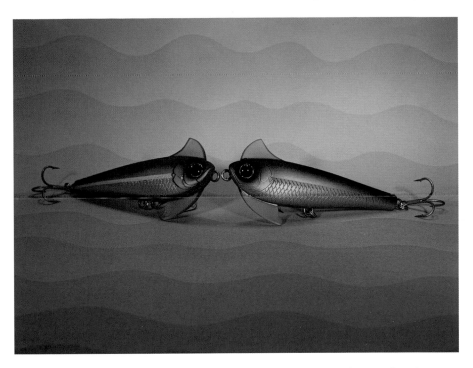

The Shimano Waxwing is an example of a modern bait that is capable of suspending when retrieved.

Those early plugs have evolved into sophisticated, fish-attracting tools. Wood and hard plastics have been joined by innovative soft plastic lures that bring an entirely new level of potential to recreational fishing both in fresh water and salt water. All forms of modern lures have advanced to a point where elements of cutting-edge science, engineering, fish physiology, and behaviors have all become integral to the design of artificial baits.

CHAPTER 2

THE RISE OF SMART BAITS

I n the world of armed conflict smart munitions are those devices that can precisely impact upon a specific target with minimal collateral damage. They are typically guided weapons capable of pinpoint accuracy, the result of sophisticated guidance systems. In essence, smart weapons differ vastly from "dumb" munitions that simply follow the cry, "bombs away!" Smart devices achieve a very specific result with a high degree of precision. That too can be said for many of today's modern artificial fishing baits.

In the world of recreational sport fishing there are a number of parallels between smart technology and contemporary fishing baits. Simply put, modern fishing baits are technologically superior to any lures that have ever been presented to fish. Some of those enhancements are attributed to the materials used in lure construction, like hi-tech, durable plastics like acrylics and other polymers, and new-age finishes that give impressions of life. Hooks are now laser sharpened to the finest points possible, and some baits anatomically replicate actual prey in appearance and movement. While older-style baits still perform with excellent results, and many are perennial favorites of freshwater and saltwater anglers alike, one has to very much appreciate the contemporary improvements of modern-age lure manufacturers that apply a new level of science to the design of their artificial baits. We are at a point in the advancement of artificial lures where there is a merging of science, technology, and art to produce unparalleled designs and quality of products offered to the angling public.

EVOLUTIONARY

Throughout the evolution of recreational fishing, artificial baits have simulated the general size, shape, and movements of natural prey. That model works well when fish are in a positive and active feeding mode. Today's high tech "smart baits" have taken that concept one very significant step further. Their designs and materials work in concert to actually "stimulate" fish to feed when they are in either neutral or non-feeding states of behavior. This is of great value to the angler, especially when one needs to maximize time on the water. Think about the possibilities. You arrive at your favorite fishing hole to only to find that the fish are off the feed, and you have a limited amount of time available for your outing. What if you could actually turn the fish on and get them to feed when they otherwise wouldn't? You might just view that as a small miracle. But that is not far from what some of today's high-tech hard and soft baits can accomplish.

A number of cutting-edge lure companies are achieving that result with their baits by precisely targeting key fish senses that are part and parcel

Smart baits appeal to all the senses of fish.

of feeding behavior driven by scent, vibrations, sight, taste, and feel. Like the precision of smart munitions of battle, the goal of a smart bait is to pinpoint the bite-triggering mechanisms in fish and motivate them to strike the lure. In practice and application some of the more sophisticated soft plastic baits can attract a fish via sight, movement, or scent, have that fish bite something that has a natural taste, and then hold on to the bait longer due to a texture and feel that replicates a real food source. The combination of those factors leads to more interest in one's baits, more strikes, and fish that hold on longer to ensure solid hook ups. Within the realm of hard plastic baits, movement, sound, and visual appeal are all enhanced by the application of state-of-the-art engineering and scientific testing. A number of manufacturers are now aggressively marketing baits referred to by the industry as reaction baits. Fundamentally, and as the name implies, those baits are designed to act as a stimulus that triggers a response. That reaction can come in the form of attraction, more aggressive strikes, greater willingness to hold a bait

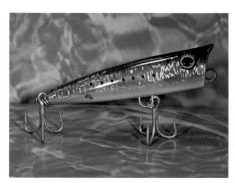 

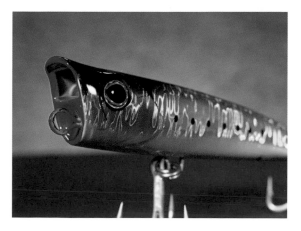

The Shimano Pop ORCA is an example of an artificial bait that appeals to multiple senses of fish. The popper is designed with an intricate depth of coloration that is visually attracting and light reflective. There is a concave portion of the head that enhances popping sounds and a unique chamber that allows for the formation of bubbles when the lure is retrieved. Those bubbles add both elements of sound and visual recognition.

once it is mouthed, and ultimately putting fish in a feeding frame of mind when they would not naturally be inclined to eat. The method by which this is achieved is to engage either some or all of the various sensory receptors of fish. In essence, fish physiology drives lure design.

APPEAL TO THE SENSES

If you want to stimulate a fish to strike your bait you must first appeal to its sensory receptors. Learn how fish react to the environment through their network of senses and you will learn how to better motivate them to accept your offerings. In general terms, fish have the ability to sense their world by acquiring critical bits of data from their watery environment. Physiologically, fish have many of the same senses as humans and other animals. Fish can see, touch, and feel. They can hear through vibrations and "smell" and "taste" through chemical receptors. Through a unique sense of electro-reception some fish, like sharks, also have the ability to sense electrical impulses given off by distressed prey and other fish.

Through millennia of evolution fish have developed a keen sense of sight. Fish use that sense much the same way as humans. Through their sight capabilities fish find food, avoid predators, find spawning mates, and even seek out shelter. From an angler's perspcctive, a fish's vision is a critical sense in finding food. Fish also have the ability to distinguish contrasting shades, to see colors, and to see in low light conditions, aided by a network of rods and cones. The obvious connection between sight and artificial baits is that what a fish can see will often get their attention, and result in further investigation. From an angler's perspective, a fish's vision is a critical sense in finding food or artificial replicas of a food source.

Fish also have the ability to "smell" via chemical reception. Through an arrangement of nostrils and an olfactory rosette, fish are able to detect and discern chemicals, often in minute quantities. In a much purer *sense* fish can actually taste through taste buds in their mouths, on their lips and tongues and faces. Some fish—like catfish—are equipped with barbels, whiskers that have feel and taste functionality. Carp are another example and utilize highly evolved and sensitive senses of smell and feel to find food. It is a fish's sense of smell that is often engaged first and attracts it to a food source.

Fish do in fact have internal ears and a lateral line that aids in the process of hearing and feeling through vibrations produced in their environment.

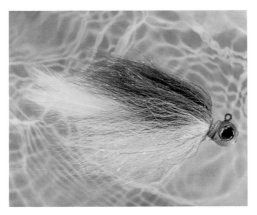

New generation bucktails like these from Premium Bucktails blend the artistry of fly tying with traditional bucktail-building techniques.

The lateral line is especially valuable in enabling a predatory fish to sense and feel the presence of other fish, prey in particular. Through rows of neuromasts (clumps of receptor cells) the lateral line helps fish navigate, avoid other fish and objects, maintain contact with other members of a school, and locate prey. The lateral line is an important element in a fish's ability to precisely locate food. It is able to detect disruptions in water like ripples that are made by struggling prey, and relay those to the brain through electrical impulses and unique nerve fibers. For the angler, baits that replicate those vibrations provide an added edge in attracting strikes.

CUTTING-EDGE SMART BAITS

Europa is the sixth moon of Jupiter. Its scientific exploration has been an intriguing undertaking. The moon was first discovered in 1610 by Galileo and named after a Phoenician noblewoman. Europa is approximately the size of our own earth's moon and is comprised mostly of silicate rock with a probable iron core. What is of interest to contemporary scientists about Europa is that is has an atmosphere composed primarily of oxygen, and it is hypothesized that beneath its surface of ice is an ocean of water that could very well support extraterrestrial marine life. Even though Galileo's discovery was made with the use of a simple twenty-power scope, the science used to support those modern conclusions is state-of-the-art, and involved the Galileo namesake space probe. The concept of extraterrestrial water and marine life got me thinking about fish right here on planet earth and how far the recreational fishing industry has come in its own right with the use of cutting-edge technology. If there was in fact water on Europa, and by some miracle of evolution, fish, my bet is that today's cutting-edge, hi-tech artificial baits would indeed catch them. And if they can do that just think about the possibilities right here on the third rock from the sun.

Many of today's leading manufacturers of plastic baits and fish-attracting scents have paid particular attention to the physiology of fish sensing mechanisms, and have applied that science to the development of new products, taking the concept of smart baits to the edge of modern technology.

Pheromone-infused baits are an example of a class of artificial baits that can stimulate feeding behavior.

Their baits work to attract fish, and in some cases actually arouse specific feeding behaviors. The technology and chemistry associated with those baits involves unique formulas of natural ingredients, known through scientific research to attract and stimulate fish to feed by releasing "feeding phero-mones." Fundamentally, pheromones are chemical stimuli that trigger a number of natural responses in animals. Pheromones play a vital role in fish physiology and behavior, from the process of reproduction and migration to fear, aggression, and behaviors associated with feeding. Specific pheromone formulas have been developed to increase the aggressive feeding behavior of fish by stimulating their natural instincts to feed. The most predominant pheromone formulas in use today are designed to trigger reactions based on fear, aggression, and feeding behaviors.

In the most fundamental ways many of the new attractants replicate the scent of a food source: baitfish, worms, crustaceans, mollusks or any other preferred prey from which scent can either be extracted or replicated. It is a simple yet ingenious concept: Create the scents that represent the food

Scents like those from BioEdge come in both liquid form and as a stick application.

which fish actually eat. At the opposite end of the spectrum, the most advanced use of attractants involves the transfer of pheromone-based scents in the form liquid mixtures in which the plastic baits are bathed. Scents can either be infused into the plastic as an integral part of the bait or contained in a liquid mix that the baits are soaked in. Experience has shown that the latter scenting method seems to have better results since the mix can be refreshed or "re-charged" and additional applications of scent can be applied to the baits as they are fished. Most all manufacturers offer sprays or soaking mixtures that can be applied to plastic baits as needed. Sometimes the application of scents can even enhance the appeal of natural baits, live or cut. The reason is that fish have protective mechanisms that can help disguise their scent by reducing the escape of bodily substances, which enable detection by predators. Applying scents to natural bait can improve and boost its effectiveness by removing masking mechanisms and allowing predators to sense the bait with greater intensity.

PLASTIC BAIT APPLICATIONS

Nowhere is this sense appeal more prevalent than in the world of soft plastic baits. Taking a look at the current landscape of plastic baits we see a wide variety of artificials that have been designed to appeal to almost all fish senses. Determining when, where, and how to apply these baits to various fishing situations will enhance one's ability to consistently catch fish. One of the very first plastic baits to gain in popularity was the plastic worm used for large-mouth bass. While there was simplicity of design with the worm, it proved to be one of the most versatile baits to hit the recreational fishing market. Depending on its rigging, it could be fished throughout the water column. Initially offered in a natural worm-like coloration, the colors expanded to an abundant array that matched the spectrum of light conditions from the surface to moderate depth levels. For the most part, the first plastic worm was a visual bait. Its soft texture was agreeable to bass; they would hold onto it longer and actually move off with like it they would with a natural bait, and this led to better hook sets. The worm's success in freshwater grabbed the attention of saltwater anglers and in early 1970s it became a popular bait along the east coast for weakfish, sea trout, and other species of the brine. An entire industry of plastic baits was spawned from the early roots of these "Creme" and "Jelly" worms. Over time, manufacturers modified the worm to

The plastic worm was one of the most revolutionary baits ever made available to anglers.

appeal not only to a fish's visual sense but also the ability to detect sound through the addition of inserted rattles, and to the sense of taste through the use of simple and natural scent additives. Salt-impregnated baits and those bathed in anise, licorice, and garlic scents certainly did motivate strikes, but those additives were more masking scents than bite stimulants. Scents applied to those early, non-absorbing plastic baits diffused rapidly, their effects diminishing quickly. More than four decades later the variety of plastic baits can be overwhelming to the typical angler, the science of their designs fascinating and their effectiveness astonishing.

Plastic baits run the gamut from fish fry sizes of one inch in length to eel sizes of fourteen inches or more, and all variations and sizes between. Plastic baits take the form of swim baits, jerk baits, stick baits, paddle tails, and tubes, including but not limited to those baits that are designed to resemble grubs, minnows, rain bait, shad, belly strips, trailers, shrimp, crawfish, lobsters, worms, flatfish, frogs, lizards, sand eels, and any assortment of aquatic and airborne creatures that fish feed on. Infinite variety is one of the benefits of soft plastic baits. In essence, the plastic molding process can replicate just about any food source that swims, crawls, or flies. With rigging variations and the application of variable weight, anglers can effectively fish plastic baits from top to bottom in the water column. The range of possibilities is best exemplified by the example that one can throw a weedless and weightless creature imitation into the lily pads for largemouth bass, or use

Plastic baits can be molded in a wide range of sizes to match prevalent bait species or fishing conditions.

a heavily-weighted ten-inch or longer jigging swim bait for cod in 220 feet of water. That range defines the meaning of versatility.

HARD BAIT INGENUITY

Hard baits, too, are designed with built-in intelligence. The way in which a plug moves to displace water affects how that plug transmits *sound* waves to

Ribbed soft baits and segmented hard baits emit greater vibrations when retrieved.

a fish's lateral line. The realistic swimming action of the bait comes as a result of the proper relationship between shape, length, and the lure's opposing forces against water. To achieve this, lure designers must closely study how fish and bait move, they way they propel themselves, and how they actually use propulsion to swim. Another critical element in lure design is that shape and balance must work in concert. The turbulence created by that balance of dimensions influences water pressure and causes the bait to move one way and then the other. The hardest thing for a lure manufacturer to understand and replicate is what fish actually feel and sense when stimulated by a particular bait. The more a hard bait is able to excite the senses, the greater its effectiveness. Contemporary smart hard baits employ a variety of design techniques to scientifically attract fish: Ribbed and segmented bodies that emit vibrations; body patterns that change color; hydro-dynamically engineered lure bodies that move with the precision of an actual baitfish; light reflection to stimulate sight responses; frequency-tuned sound devices; and even lures and devices equipped with built-in light emitting capabilities that generate color that is specific to certain fishing depths.

The array of today's hard baits is amazingly broad for both freshwater and saltwater game fish. Lures that are now on the market are versatile and in many ways designed to target specific behaviors of game fish and the baitfish they pursue. Modern hard plastic baits are revolutionary in their action, their appeal to the sensory networks of fish, the use of realistic finishes, and the way in which they can be fished throughout the water column. The contemporary concept is to engineer lures that can stimulate multiple fish senses as the angler retrieves and manipulates the lure. Once a fish is aroused by the action of the bait, the goal is to elicit not only feeding strikes but reaction strikes as well. Predatory fish depend heavily on their sense of sight to zone in on their prey. Even when sound or smell is a fish's first sense to kick into gear, it is usually the sense of sight that seals the deal when stalking prey. Most game fish are sight feeders but their other senses, when stimulated, will guide the predators to within range of their prey. Fundamentally, these new hard baits will attract fish via sound, motion, visual appeal, and in some instances smell. Popping noises can be created during the retrieve. Rattles can be installed into the interior of plugs to generate constant sound when the lure is in motion. And design techniques

Modern lure designs are innovative in their capacity to motivate strikes.

can allow for a range of motion that goes well beyond the standards of float-ing and sinking.

One of the most innovative design features of modern hard baits allows for the lures to both descend and then suspend in the water column. This capability has significant value in that it allows the angler to precisely and methodically fish a substantial amount of vertical water, and then manipu-late lure within the zone in which fish are found. Suspended freshwater bass are a typical target of this style of fishing but even saltwater game fish will hang in the water column where prey species are also present. A lure that can

The use of modern materials gives contemporary bucktails diversity of size, shape, profile, and color.

be consistently fished in that zone will yield more strikes. Another example of that kind of versatility is the timeless bucktail, which today is a far cry from the bucktails of old. What was once a simple lead head on a hook with deer bucktail tied in on the shaft has transformed into a modern work of art. Builders of bucktails now use realistic heads, laser-sharpened hooks, 3-D and holographic eyes, and natural and synthetic materials for tails. And some of these baits are now tied to replicate various fly patterns, creating the possibility to imitate a wide range of natural baits. In their most primitive form bucktails are still effective baits, but by incorporating modern materials and more hydrodynamic concepts into their designs, these baits have transformed into "smart" baits.

One major reality with fishing is that no matter how effective or smart a contemporary artificial bait may be, the key variable in the equation is the angler acting to exert influence on the line and lure, in order to make it behave in a natural and realistic way. The sophistication of smart baits give the angler a major advantage over the fish species they target. These baits will work in concert with one's fishing skills to dramatically increase the consistency of the catch.

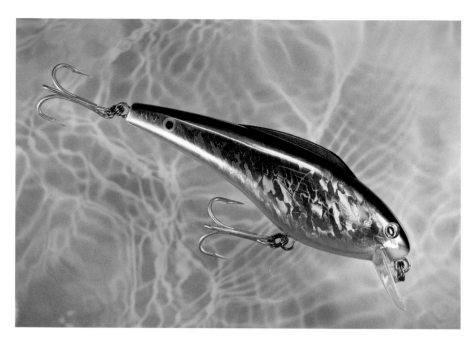

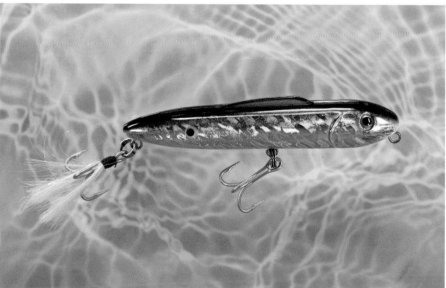

Holographic finishes like the one on these Guide's Secret baits reflect light in a manner that can attract fish to strike.

CHAPTER 3

THE SCIENCE OF FISHING...AND CATCHING

In a purely literal sense, science is a knowledge-based discipline, partly skill and partly art. According to the definition in the Merriam Webster dictionary, science represents knowledge about or study of the natural world based on facts learned through experiments and observation. We can also apply that same discipline to the pursuit of fishing, especially since the paths of science and fishing often cross. While there is something to be said for returning to the good old days of a cane pole, a can of earth worms, a bobber and some bluegills, there is no escaping the fact that today's successful anglers depend as much on science and technology as they do on their acquired fishing skills. The modern reality is that those who fish recreationally encounter the results of scientific inquiry at every phase of the game: Rod blanks manufactured from high-density carbon fibers and space-age nano resins; strong and light titanium reels; super-efficient lines designed for diverse applications; intelligent artificial lures that appeal to all of a fish's senses and that are often more effective than live bait; and electronics that can figuratively pinpoint with astonishing accuracy a pimple on the snout of a striped bass swimming in one hundred feet of water. Beyond the tackle and gear, science helps explain not only the behaviors of bait and baitfish, but also the inter-relationship of other key factors like tides, weather, and water quality.

Dr. Dave Ross is an oceanographer, and a Senior Scientist Emeritus at the Woods Hole Oceanographic Institution in Massachusetts. He is the author of numerous scientific textbooks and he also wrote, *The Fisherman's Ocean: How Marine Science Can Help You Find and Catch More Fish*. In his book, Dr. Ross describes marine environments and ecosystems and the behavior of saltwater fish. To the benefit of anglers, Dr. Ross further explores the factors that stimulate fish to act in specific ways—the effects of their senses on how they hear, smell, taste, and see; how that translates to actions and responses; how they migrate and where they amass; and how they travel with currents and tides. As Dr. Ross explains: "Fish, to me, are very complex creatures, many having some senses that exceed ours in ability. For example, most fish can detect a scent literally a thousand times better than a dog. The ocean is very noisy, but most fish can still distinguish and detect sounds from bait or predators. Using and knowing scientific information about fish and their environment may help you to find and hook more fish, but even if it doesn't it should make your time on the water more enjoyable, and make you appreciate fish even more." Dr. Ross is also a very seasoned and accomplished angler who has researched and fished in many of the world's oceans. In his view fish have remarkable sensory mechanisms and strong abilities to detect and distinguish motion, noise, color and scent. When translating those traits into useable fishing knowledge Dr. Ross suggests that an artificial lure's ability to imitate sick or dying prey is a critical design element in getting the attention of fish. Dr. Ross further adds that it is important for an angler to understand the physiology and behaviors not only of the game fish they pursue, but of the bait as well. While replicating anatomical accuracy in an artificial bait is not critical, Dr. Ross suggests that understanding the impact of how a fish sees, hears, and detects scent is of utmost importance to anglers.

The simple fact that many successful contemporary anglers have embraced principles of science to up their game and increase cast-to-catch ratios cannot be argued. Take, for example, Greg Myerson, the current IGFA all-tackle striped bass world record holder. His bass of 81.88 pounds is indeed a magnificent specimen of the species and an extraordinary bass in a long line of gargantuan fish caught by one of the most prolific big bass experts along the entirety of the east and west coasts. Consistency of this magnitude does not occur by happenstance but by a lot of hard work, time on the water, and an understanding of big bass habits and physiology. Trophies of Myerson's caliber simply don't behave like school-size bass. Among all the strategies and tactics Myerson employs to target super-large striped bass, his practice of applying scientific insights to his fishing approach helps stack the deck in his favor. His proven belief is to appeal to all the senses of large bass. According to Myerson, "I would tell anglers that in my experience fish hunt in this order: Sound first, smell second, and sight third, using their eyes only for the final attack." So what does this all have to do with him catching monster striped bass? Myerson depends on sound technology as much as he does his rod and reel and has taken that science to the point of using and patenting certain sounds made by prey that striped bass feed on. He has also extended the decibel levels and frequencies of those sounds to his lures, baits, and terminal gear since he also believes that bass can distinguish between the sounds made by different prey. In the final analysis, Greg's methods and tactics are rooted in sound science and fish anatomy, and the results he achieves speak volumes about the effectiveness of his fishing. Myerson's achievements with especially large striped bass are legendary and his advice regarding lure selection for catching large specimens of any species is invaluable: "Big fish are much harder to fool. You need the most natural presentations. The best size lines and fluorocarbons for the clarity of the water.

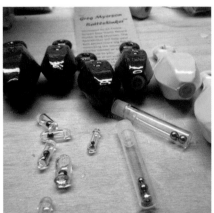

World striped bass record holder, Greg Myerson, believes strongly in the influence of specific sound in getting big bass to bite. Photo Credit: Greg Myerson.

The right twitches and bumps. Color scheme and most importantly the lure has to sound like something the fish recognize as food. Not just *noise*—they will be less likely to strike something that they don't understand as food. The twenties might hit them, but not sixty-plus pounders that have been around the block a few times!" Myerson has taken his proven beliefs and tactics well beyond personal fishing and into the realm of business with the founding of the World Record Striper Company. Through this enterprise he shares his knowledge and products that use proprietary sound technology to attract fish to his baits. Myerson's flagship product is the trademarked "Rattlesinker" that incorporates tiny beads to create unique vibrations that stimulate the sound-sensing lateral lines in a variety of fish. According to Myerson, his technique, referred to as "Rattling," involves bouncing his unique sinker up and down and in contact with the bottom to produce subsonic vibrations that stimulate the sense of sound in fish and cause them to seek out the source of the sound; once attracted to sound, the fish can zero in on bait.

As we have seen, fish fundamentally also have the ability to "smell" via chemical reception. Through an arrangement of nostrils and an olfactory rosette, fish are able to detect and distinguish chemicals, often in minute quantities. Fish can actually taste through taste buds on their mouths, lips, tongues, and faces. Targeting a fish's senses of smell and taste is at the fore-front of modern, science-based lure design. A number of years ago while researching an article on smart baits and lures, I had the opportunity to interview John Prochnow, who was the Product Development Director at Pure Fishing and one of the innovators of the Gulp! line of soft baits and scent baths. His comments warrant repeating since they summarized the Gulp! approach to stimulating sensory mechanisms in fish. "Our baits target and stimulate all response sections within fish and are designed to maximize scent and flavor, texture, action, and vibration and cosmetic appeal such as color and profile. Under normal conditions when fish are in a somewhat neutral or feeding mode it is important for all those artificial bait elements to work in concert. There are conditions when one or more of those elements might prevail. For example, in muddy or dingy water a bait that appeals to a fish's ability to sense scent and vibration is most effective; in clear water appealing to visual acuity is key. Flavor and texture tend to be the last of the elements put into play since at that point a fish has already been attracted to the artificial bait."

Products like
Berkley Gulp!
target the sensory
mechanisms in
fish that stimulate
feeding activity.

One critical characteristic of successful artificial baits is an inherent capacity to create the perception of live food or injured and vulnerable prey. All artificial lures, whether hard or soft baits, are in essence deceptive imposters of a real food source that is impaired in some form or is an otherwise healthy target. The more capable the imitation is of replicating something that appears alive and susceptible, the more receptive game fish will be to strike. Artificial baits with high "imposter quotients" are likely to draw more interest and, therefore, more strikes. Learn how fish react to the environment through their network of senses and you will learn how to better motivate them to accept your artificial offerings. Chris Paparo does exactly that. Paparo has a degree in marine biology and is a senior aquarist, diver, and the manager of Stony Brook University's Marine Research Laboratory in Southampton. He is also known as the "Fish Guy" for his extensive knowledge of local and migratory fish species and the marine environments that surround Long Island, New York. Paparo also knows the value of incorporating science into his outdoor endeavors. As an avid angler, Chris's professional career and his recreational fishing pursuits often intersect. And as a diver and marine photographer, Paparo regularly observes fish up close and in their natural state and documents their behavior. His observations have led to changes in the way he fishes. According to Paparo, "Having a better understanding of fish behavior through study and observation has allowed me to think more like a fish. Knowing how a fish might react under certain circumstances (i.e., tide, current, time of day, etc.). gives me an edge in knowing not only what lure or bait to use, but how to properly apply it." Paparo suggests that:

> We are often taught various fishing techniques without ever fully understanding why those methods are successful. For example, when targeting fluke, it is best to fish along sandbars. Why is this so? As an ambush predator, fluke will lie on the bottom, facing into the current while waiting for baitfish to be swept over the bar. As a diver, I have seen fluke work the slope of a sandbar. With this knowledge, I know where to present my lure to increase my odds that it will flutter past the mouth of a hungry fluke. Another example would be fishing for blackfish. Blackfish are tied to structure, but not all pieces of the wreck will hold fish at all stages of the tide. During times of slow water, blackfish will cruise the wreck looking for prey. As currents increase, they will often take shelter behind large objects and will wait for food to come to them. When currents are strong, I try to get my rig to drift behind objects such as pilings of boulders where the big tautog are waiting out the tide.

This marriage of scientific observation with angling technique can only lead to greater fishing success. It is the wise angler who continually observes the environment, baitfish and game fish behavior, and seeks to understand critical interrelationships, and then apply that knowledge to his or her fishing tactics.

Many of today's leading lure manufacturers design and engineer their soft and hard baits with built-in "intelligence" that appeals to the entire spectrum of fish senses and physiology. Similarly, tackle manufacturers use the most sophisticated materials to create the strongest, lightest, and most responsive fishing rods ever used by fishermen. Some reels have compounds that are more advanced than those in some aircraft. The realistic swimming action of artificial baits results from the proper relationship between shape, length and the lure's opposing forces against water. To achieve this, lure designers study how fish and bait move, they way they propel themselves, and how they use propulsion to swim. Another critical element in lure design is shape and balance that must work in concert. The turbulence

As a fisherman and a diver, Chris Paparo gleans lessons from above and below the water. Credit: Chris Paparo.

created by that balance of dimensions influences water pressure and causes the bait to move one way and then the other. The hardest thing for a lure manufacturer to understand and replicate is what fish actually feel and sense when stimulated by a particular bait. It is the truly smart angler that absorbs this kind of relevant information from any and all sources. Roy Leyva is one such fisherman. His consistent and often uncanny ability to catch a wide range of fish species from Maine to Florida has earned Roy a well-deserved reputation as a master angler. He is one of core of savvy fishermen who have embraced the wide-ranging benefits of science. Roy's take on the impact of science to his fishing: "Braided lines have revolutionized everything! From rods to reels and lures. And new plastic materials have had a huge impact on durability and lifelike appearance of artificial baits. Computer programs now can design baits to cast farther, work differently, and swim much like a natural bait fish."

Contemporary tackle manufacturing employs a variety of design techniques to scientifically attract fish: Ribbed and segmented lure bodies emit vibrations, body patterns change color, hydrodynamic lure bodies move with the precision of an actual baitfish, light reflection stimulates sight responses, suspending stick and jerk baits, frequency-tuned sound devices, and even lures and devices equipped with built-in light emitting capabilities generate color specific to the depths fished. And now rod builders use nanofibers that add magic to fishing rods.

An example of how the lines of science and the lines of fishing intersect can be seen at Long Island's Brookhaven National Laboratory. The laboratory's Center for Functional Nanomaterials (CFN) explores the unique properties of materials and processes at the nanoscale. Scott Bronson, Manager of BNL's K-12 Educational Programs explains that "the CFN hosts a broad range of research investigations in nanoscience. However, the main focus has been on topics related to basic energy science—exploring more efficient catalysts for fuel cells, developing organic solar thin films, and finding new ways to combine nanoparticles to create multifunctional materials." As a fisherman, Bronson does acknowledge that the broader field of

Scott Bronson sees the impact that nanotechnology is having on recreational fishing. Credit: Scott Bronson.

nanotechnology is having an impact on the sport fishing industry, especially in the development of nanoparticle-containing resins used in advanced graphite rod manufacturing. Even so, he believes that material science applied to fishing rods seems to be a balancing act of trade-offs. "I have nano-resins in my graphite saltwater surf and fly rods, yet I still prefer the older technology of bamboo when fly fishing the Carmans River for brook trout." In essence, the application drives the choice of materials used or the technology employed.

Beyond the use of nanoresins, a revolutionary material, rod builders are now considering graphene as a superior material as well for rod building. Graphene is a film-like, single-carbon atom layer. Pound-for-pound it is almost one hundred times stronger than steel. Although semiconductor and electronics industries now primarily use grapheme, graphene has caught the attention of some enterprising folks in the fishing industry. The flexing capability of graphene and the ability of the material to store and release energy efficiently represent beneficial characteristics when designing fly rods with increased power, distance, and accuracy.

As technology engages in its perpetual quest for change and improvement, the fishing industry will continue to benefit from those advancements. Whether old science or new, understanding the impact of science on your fishing and embracing that science in your angling repertoire will have remarkable results.

CHAPTER 4

PRIME-TIME PLASTICS

In the movie classic *The Graduate*, a young Dustin Hoffman has a career discussion with one Mr. McGuire while the infamous Mrs. Robinson attempts to seduce the young man. McGuire offers Hoffman's character, Benjamin, one word of worldly business advice: "Plastics." While Benjamin was much more focused on the seduction by Mrs. Robinson, the reference to the fast-growing plastics industry was right on the mark. Plastics in their many forms transformed manufacturing and brought a multiplicity of beneficial products to the American public. Notwithstanding that magnitude of change, even the recreational fishing industry was a prime beneficiary of the plastics revolution. At first the applications involved the manufacture of hard baits that had for decades been made from wood. Those plastic baits were a huge success since they were highly effective, easy to manufacture, and readily available. But over time, the technology for producing plastic lures changed, and soft plastic baits opened new possibilities. Those soft baits in their seemingly limitless forms changed the way many anglers fish.

Since the Creme Worm was introduced to the freshwater bass-fishing world in 1949, soft, pliable baits have been a staple in tackle boxes worldwide for both freshwater and saltwater fishing. From simple baits to more exotic formulas, plastics have caught countless species of fish around the globe, and in all their forms have become go-to confidence baits. The reasons are easy to understand. First and foremost, plastic can be molded, and when a fish grabs hold of a soft plastic bait it holds on longer since the feel is more realistic than that of a hard bait.

Plastics are ideal polymers for the manufacture of artificial fishing into boundless profiles, shapes, and sizes, replicating an even more limitless number of prey baits, swimming seductively in the water and replicating the exact movements of their natural counterparts. Many of their properties are very suitable for the way lures function. For example, most plastics withstand the effects of water, especially saltwater, and resist corrosion. Plastics

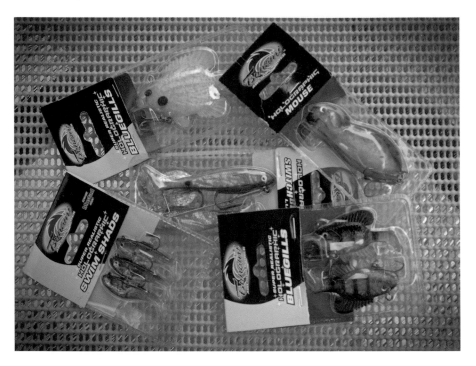

Modern soft plastic baits are available in an almost limitless array of variations.

also have high strength-to-weight relationships and are very durable. Contemporary soft bait engineering is creating stronger materials while retaining pliability and resilience. Plastics are very robust and wear hard, even under harsh conditions like those encountered in the surf, around rocks and boulders, and when fishing offshore. Both hard and soft plastics can also be fabricated in a limitless array of colors, and are also ideal for integrating fish-attracting options. Scent is a very important factor in a fish's ability to find various concentrations of bait fish. From tiny twister tails for bluegills to enormous soft baits for offshore fishing, appropriately-applied scents can increase angler hook-up percentages. Even fundamental sight feeders will often first locate prey by initially zoning-in on the scent released by those masses of bait. The soft plastic medium can retain scents and act as a vessel for rattle inserts and other noisemakers. By doing so these baits can appeal to the entire scope of fish senses, and that means more interest from fish and ultimately more strikes.

Throughout the evolution of recreational fishing, lure makers have designed and fabricated plastic baits to simulate the general size, shape, and

The plastic molding process allows for great variations in designs.

movements of natural prey. That model works well when fish are in a positive and active feeding mode. Today's high tech soft baits have taken that concept one very significant step further. Their designs and materials work in concert to actually stimulate fish to feed when they are in either neutral or non-feeding feeding states of behavior. When the angler's skill at manipulating a soft bait to mimic natural movements of prey is added to the equation we have a very powerful combination of influences at work to lure fish. The

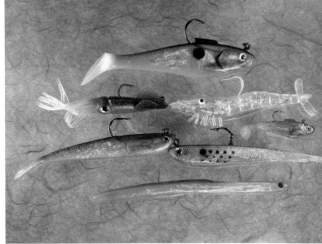

The plastic molding process can yield lifelike size, shape, and feel to soft plastic baits.

Modern smart baits embody many elements of realism.

sophistication of plastic baits certainly provides for a major advantage over the fish species that are targeted. The baits can work in concert with one's fishing acumen to dramatically increase catch ratios and consistency of catch. Soft plastic baits are also ideal reaction baits. Fundamentally, and as the name implies, those baits are designed to act as a stimulus that triggers a response. That reaction can come in the form of attraction, more aggressive strikes, greater holding power once a bait is mouthed, and ultimately putting fish in a feeding frame of mind when they would not naturally be inclined to eat.

One significant characteristic of soft plastic is their ability to retain either imbedded or applied scent. This opens up a whole new world of baits that for all practical purposes are prime time baits regardless of the season or species. The reasons are simple. Many of today's leading manufacturers of plastic baits and fish attracting scents have paid particular attention to the physiology of fish sensing mechanisms and have applied that science to the development of new products, taking the concept of soft baits and scents to the edge of modern technology. Their baits work to attract fish, and in some cases can actually "stimulate" fish to feed. I have personally enjoyed considerable success using scent infused soft plastic baits on many species of fish and the results have been very impressive. For saltwater species like summer flounder, sea bass, and porgies, those types of baits can at times be more effective than natural bait. In fresh water, wary and reluctant carp have also been willing to eat diminutive soft plastic tails that have been soaked in scent.

One such product type is Berkley Gulp! At the time I spoke with John Prochnow, he was the Product Development Director at Pure Fishing, and I was working on a series of articles about modern baits for a regional fishing magazine. John was also one of the lead developers for the innovative and highly effective Berkley Gulp! soft baits. In some fishing circles Gulp! soft baits have attained a status as a bait that is at times even more useful and effective than natural bait. Just ask anyone who fishes for summer flounder, also known as fluke. I know that where I fish on Long Island most fluke anglers regularly use Gulp!, some almost exclusively. The first question I asked John was what makes Gulp! products so irresistible to fish? It was a simple question with a not-so-simple an answer. "There are multiple reasons but a key feature is that the materials matrix of our soft baits is water-based polymer. That allows for faster dispersion of water-soluble scents and attractants." John then referenced a quick history of "plastic" baits. "First there was rubber, and then PVC (polyvinyl chloride), and now we have water-based materials." According to Prochnow this allows the bait to first act as a sponge holding the scents and attractants, and then facilitates faster

Scented baits like Berkley Gulp! appeal to a fish's sense of smell.

and more effective dispersion of scent into the water. The previous rubber and PVC generations of soft baits contained the scent and even locked it. As water diffuses through a Gulp! product, it allows the scented attractants to more efficiently and effectively flow into the environment. John added, "What this allows for is a broader strike zone for fish to first detect and then zone in on the bait. Water-soluble baits are much more effective at allowing scents to disperse."

Prochnow further explained that cutting-edge baits like Gulp! are designed with a "full-line" approach to stimulating all response sections within fish. What that means is those baits are designed to maximize scent and flavor, texture, action, and vibration, as well as cosmetic appeal such as color and profile. Which of those elements is most important? John replied that generally, under normal conditions when fish are in a somewhat neutral or feeding mode, it is important for all those plastic bait elements to work in concert. Yet, John added, there are conditions when one or more of those elements might prevail. For example in muddy or dingy water, a bait that appeals to a fish's ability to sense scent and vibration is most effective; in clear water appealing to visual acuity is key. Flavor and texture tend to be the last of the elements put into play, since at that point a fish has already noticed and struck the lure. John also indicated that research has shown that the variables change depending on the species. Some fish may be stimulated more by one of the elements than another, and that can further change based upon other environmental factors.

John also indicated that the design process for soft baits is somewhat more complex than that of hard baits, since there are many more variables and subtleties of design. While the action of hard baits can be evaluated in float tanks on the factors of sway, surge, roll, yaw, pitch, and heave, that is more problematic with soft baits. Yet, they work to duplicate hard bait design disciplines into their line of soft baits. Furthermore, they computer model all their baits and "fish" them with a robotic angler in a laboratory setting with real fish before field testing under live fishing conditions. This enables them to see how the fish react to and strike specific lures. Laboratory testing of chemical reception has a high degree of predictability for real-life situations. In John's words, the predictability is "uncanny." As far as the next generation of soft baits, John foresees new-age raw materials further enhancing the effectiveness of the current crop of baits. He also offers this tip to anglers who fish scented plastic baits: "Fish them slower to allow the scent to disperse and leave a trail; the fish will respond better."

Peter Cowin is the founder and president of BioEdge, a manufacturer of fishing scents. I've spoken with Cowin to understand his brand philosophy and to gain insight into his knowledge of the interrelationship between scent and fishing success. His wisdom in that regard is intriguing. According to Cowin, "Decades of scientific research has established the remarkable capacity for fish to detect scents in parts per million, sometimes per billion. Millions of years of evolution enable fish to detect injured prey from hundreds of yards away or to locate bait in near zero visibility. BioEdge scents are made from real bait using a unique cold extraction process. They capture the complex and delicate mixture of natural bait oils, enzymes, and pheromones from real bait and package it in a form which can be applied to any kind of lure or used to enhance cut bait, making it more easily detected and more readily attacked by most fish species." Peter added that tests conducted with scent-treated baits reveal a four- to six-times advantage over untreated lures or bait. The most remarkable finding of those tests reveals that even natural bait, when treated with enhanced scent, is more effective than without. Regarding oil-based scents, Peter explains that often what you do not see is important. "As the oil droplets travel up to the surface they are releasing soluble scents all the way to the surface, far, far faster than they would be dispersed when only water-based components are used, dispersing scent throughout the whole water column."

I also asked Peter to peer into the crystal ball and tell what he sees regarding the next generation of plastic baits, scents, and other attractants. Combining his experiences as a trained marine zoologist and as a manufacturer of fish attractants, Peter's response was fascinating. "There are several ways that I see artificial baits moving in the next decade: I see lure manufacturers incorporating what is known as a 'super stimulus'—a built-in reaction mechanism inside the brains of many animals and fish which trigger response even better than that which is used in the wild." An example of this was presented in a classic work by Nobel Laureate, Nikolaas Tinbergen, in his 1951 Study of Instinct. Territorial male sticklebacks aggressively strike a wooden float according to the degree of the redness of the paint on the float. Another example of a super stimulus is a specific pattern of color that triggers response more so than a single color.

Peter further postulated on the future of scent attractants: "There is a great rush in the lure industry to infuse feeding stimulants to lures. I see this diversifying as more companies try to imitate the natural chemical queues fish use to find prey. Our technique is to use those that nature makes, but plenty of man-made alternatives will be presented to anglers with claims of being just as good or better. But my money is on backing the queues evolved over millions of years." Two other areas of stimuli that Peter speculated about are electrical and vibration: "We are just scratching the surface of using lures with an electromagnetic field detectable by many fish species. There will be a lot of these lures on the market soon." Regarding vibration, "Whether this is achieved by physical rattles or computer chips, lures with more realistic or irresistible vibration will become more common."

In the most basic ways many of the new attractants replicate the scent of a food source: baitfish, worms, crustaceans, mollusks, or any other preferred prey from which scent can either be extracted or replicated. It is a simple yet ingenious concept: Create the scents that represent the food which fish actually eat. At the opposite end of the spectrum, the most advanced use

Liquid potions like those of BioEdge enhance the appeal of artificial baits.

of attractants involves the transfer of pheromone-based scents in liquid mixtures to bathe the plastic baits.

Plastic baits can be fished effectively during any season of the year and for most any fish whose feeding zone can be reached with the soft baits. In some form they are prime-time baits any time of the year. On the New York saltwater scene, soft plastics are highly effective on striped bass, fluke, sea bass, scup, Atlantic bonito, little tunny, and bluefish tuna. In freshwater the choices are even greater. I don't think you can find a largemouth or smallmouth bass angler anywhere in this country who doesn't have at least one tackle bag totally dedicated to soft baits. Scent only can work to enhance the

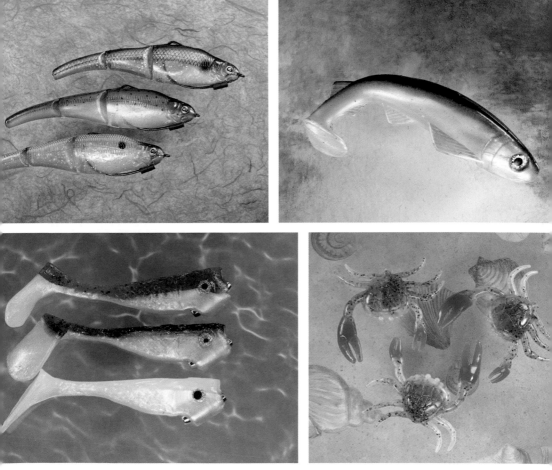

The hallmark of soft plastic baits is the variety of natural bait forms they can replicate.

effectiveness of soft plastic baits. Many anglers are so confident in scented soft baits that they use those baits in lieu of natural ones, and that trend is spreading. There are certainly times and situations when fish respond better to natural offerings, but as technology improves the texture, taste, and action of soft plastic baits, those artificial lures will prevail.

As effective as contemporary plastic baits are, the key variable in the equation is the angler as he or she acts to exert influence on the line and lure to make it behave in a natural and realistic way. The sophistication of smart baits give the angler a major advantage over the fish species they target, and can work in concert with one's fishing skills to dramatically increase the consistency of the catch. A number of years ago I had the opportunity to fish one of the best smallmouth bass rivers in the northeast. I had stayed at a lodge and chose to cut the learning curve for the area by fishing with a friend who was, at the time, a local guide. As I loaded my gear into his large Grand Laker canoe he said to me that he needed to stop for some bait. "We need live minnows to catch these bass." I responded by saying that I did not want bait but would prefer to fish artificials. He insisted on the minnows. By day's end we had boated countless smallmouth bass up to a few nice five-pound fish, and not a single one was taken on a live minnow. All fish were caught on a variety of soft plastic baits. The next time we fished, there was no mention of minnows. And the following year on my return to that same river my guide friend had an entire tackle box of soft baits, and talked endlessly of their virtues. Such is the fascination with and appeal of prime-time plastics.

CHAPTER 5

CROSSOVER BAITS

A number of decades back, crossover vehicles became the rage of the auto industry. To a great extent they still are. These cars were hybrids of sorts resulting from a cross between SUVs and family sedans. Consumers loved the amenities and ride of a traditional automobile and the muscle and all-wheel-drive of an SUV. It was a marriage made in heaven so successful that it spawned an entire new genre of vehicles that have endured the test of time. But cars are not the only form of hybrid crossover that have had success. The fishing industry followed the lead of their car-making counterparts and created artificial lures that do double duty in both fresh water and salt water. The fishing industry has also been a beneficiary of similar innovative engineering and production techniques that expand the potential of artificial lures, which opens up new opportunities for anglers, especially those who fish for both freshwater and saltwater species. In much the same way that hybrid automobiles perform a dual purpose, crossover lures can function effectively for multiple species in different environments. When combined with new-age technology and science-based lure design techniques, crossover baits offer substantial benefits over single-purpose artificial lures.

My angling roots are firmly entrenched in freshwater fishing, and I never stray too far from the light tackle lessons garnered from those experiences. Aside from some youthful forays with winter flounder, eels, and tomcod, largemouth bass offered my first real exposure to sport fishing. That was more than five decades ago, yet the influences of freshwater bass permeate throughout all my present-day saltwater fishing activities. I am far from being alone in that regard. Many anglers I know have traveled a similar path, and have a fishing lineage that also extends back to bluegills, bass, and trout, and time spent honing skills on lakes, ponds, streams, and rivers. When I first entered into the saltwater side of the fishing game, many of the larger lures that I used for bass and other species initially followed me into

Poppers like this one from Guide's Secret utilize design, coloration and embedded sound that appeal to multiple fish senses.

the brine. I enjoyed many successful outings with those lures until I began to acquire artificial baits that were specific to saltwater use. For example, many of the plugs that were used for largemouth bass, pike, muskies, and salmon also performed well for various saltwater species like striped bass, bluefish, and weakfish. And in some instances the reverse was also true with small versions of saltwater baits yielding excellent results in freshwater for both largemouth and smallmouth bass. I had an intriguing experience that drives this point home.

During the mid-1990s the mid-Atlantic and northeast regions of the East Coast of the United States experienced a dramatic resurgence in the stocks of striped bass. That explosive expansion of the species was of a magnitude that the ranks of anglers throughout the range of striped bass swelled to unprecedented numbers. Opportunities to catch quality bass along the entire coast were not only available to traditional surf and boating anglers, but were such that they produced a significant saltwater fly-fishing industry and a new cadre of light-tackle and fly-fishing guides. I had the opportunity to fish a section of the Rhode Island coastline for striped bass with one such angler. My host was an interesting captain. This part-time guide was a full-time veterinarian. He was also a man of science, and fishing with him was akin to taking a three-credit course in biology and animal behavior. Not only did he prove to be a terrific angler but also a source of substantive angling wisdom. After three days of fishing I boated and released my fair share of quality striped bass on the fly. I also added valuable insights to my tackle box of knowledge. At every opportunity my host would take time to point out the behavioral significance of what each fish told us—lessons from those that were caught, and those that were not. At one point during that outing we hit upon an area that the captain had talked about all throughout the trip. It was a seasonal honey hole that had just recently turned on. It had been his bread and butter guide spot over the past several charters, and in his words, a "no fail zone." But much to my dismay, we could not draw a single strike on flies from that spot despite covering the entire water column with different lines and various size and color fly patterns. The captain was not at all stymied by this but rather said simply, "Time to do what the bass pros do."

"And what is that?" I asked.

"Experiment. They make their living fishing and they are always experimenting with different baits and techniques. I follow their lead—do what they do." And so it was that we too experimented, throwing freshwater rattling lures, swimming plugs, top-water plugs, and soft plastics baits until we dialed in on what the bass wanted that day. In the end, there were stripers in that honey hole and we eventually got them to eat baits that were originally designed for largemouth bass.

I've thought about that experience many times since, and one time in particular a few seasons back while motoring out of my homeport in the central Long Island Sound. I was inching my way out of the harbor when something under one of the boat docks caught my eye: there was a splash and some nervous water. I swung the boat back around and turned off the engine. Picking up a fly rod, I tossed a few casts to the dock and let the fly sink. No takers. I tried a few more casts that proved futile and put the rod down. I then grabbed a spinning rod rigged with a swimming plug and made a few more casts back into the deeper recesses of the dock. Despite some uneasy water indicative of baitfish movement, there still were no takers. By now my boat had drifted well off from the dock pilings. I was getting ready to move on when I asked myself the question: "If the back of this harbor were a freshwater lake and if those docks were the only available structure, what would bass pros do right now?" Then it hit me: They'd "flip and pitch." I reached for yet another rod in my arsenal and re-rigged it with a very modern largemouth bass bait. This tube-and-tail style lure had it all: the proven attributes of a jig, undulating legs, a soft plastic body infused with scents, a rattle, and an appealing color. The lure had potential appeal to all the senses of a fish.

This hybrid-type bait somewhat resembled a small, non-descript crustacean. A guide friend in Maine had nicknamed the contraption the "Bomb-Basst." It is a proven killer on big down-east smallmouth bass. Over the years I've used that lure in different sizes and color combinations for catching a wide range of fish. The overall weight of the lure was a little more than half an ounce, and under the circumstance that confronted me, I flipped it along the side of the dock that had revealed signs of life. With that cast I had "crossed-over" and was fishing for saltwater striped bass using a freshwater bass lure and technique. The bait fluttered down and I fished it as if trying to lure a big old bucketmouth from among a tangle of lily pads and stumps. I bounced that bait around, knocked at the dock, and a striped bass was indeed home. While this was not the first time that I had used freshwater artificial baits for saltwater fish, it was one of those epiphany moments when the light bulb went on and reinforced the virtues of experimentation. The difference this time was that the bait tied to the end of my line was significantly more "intelligent" than the older lures in my tackle box.

The Pig 'n' Jig combination has become a an extremely effective bait for largemouth bass
Credit: Greg Kiessling..

When one considers crossover baits in the context of modern lures, it is relatively easy to make the leap from a standard bait to one that is "smart." Take for instance the tube-and-tail combination that I flipped and pitched for striped bass. By marrying the best attributes of a jig to the appeal of a scented soft plastic tube and tail, I created the best of multiple worlds. The combined effects of that bait's characteristics would work in concert to stimulate several sensory mechanisms that fish use to find prey. The forward-positioned weight at the head of the bait allows for a jigging action that fish often find irresistible; the scented soft body motivates fish to not only bite the bait but to hang on to it; the rattle appeals to a fish's senses of hearing via the lateral line; and the plastic legs and coloration act as visual stimulants as a predatory fish moves in for the final assault. There are so many varieties of plastics on the market today that all one needs to do is experiment. I have had striped bass take any assortment of atypical plastic lures: Hellgrammites, crawfish imitations, lizards, and even frog-shaped designs—each integrated as a trailer with a tube lure. Colors and sizes can be mixed and matched to create a reasonable facsimile of prevalent bait. One of the better producers for me when employing flipping and pitching techniques is a red-and-white tube combination with a tentacle-type collar and a large plastic grub as a trailer, and fished just like a jig. That half-ounce package comes pretty close to resembling small squid. The aerodynamics of tubes allows them to be cast and skipped into places otherwise inaccessible using other lure types. A tube lure will fall with a side-to side motion, creating the appearance of wounded bait. An additional benefit of tube lures and other similar baits, is that manufacturers infuse all sorts of fishy scents and salty tastes into the plastic. It is believed that these attributes aid in causing bass to hold onto the artificial longer as if it were the real thing. It seems to work. Pitching and skipping tube lure combinations around and under docks and along piers is a great way to attract the attention of any game fish that may be holding in those types of areas. Retrieving the tube by skipping it and then allowing the bait to sink and flutter down on a slack line is often more than a hungry striper can handle.

Some of the first flipping lures were tube-and-tail combinations with varying size bullet weights, usually in the range of a half to about 1.5 ounces. For saltwater use I prefer baits of one half to three quarter ounces. Line should be on the heavy side since fish are hooked at close range and you often have

Jigs like the Shimano Lucanus are very effective for bottom and near-bottom dwelling species. The jig incorporates many of the best features of both saltwater and freshwater baits.

to pull them out from structure. Low-diameter, high-test braid is an ideal choice. Hybrid lines also work well for this application. While this is a fairly straightforward technique for largemouth bass, it takes a little more practice with striped bass, but it can be accomplished if the fish are moderately sized and relate to tight structure. The method works best if fish are holding in a location rather than moving through an area. Another key to success is to position the boat as close to the structure as possible; a quiet approach is essential. Traditional bucktail combinations with the addition of either plastic tails or pork rind are productive, yet I have had my best fishing with various tube lure combinations that are ideal for this style of fishing.

Although crossover baits have moved along a two-way street, it has been the freshwater lures that initially made the transition to salt water. And in many respects artificial lures designed for largemouth bass were the first to serve a dual purpose. One of the best examples of this is the plastic worm, specifically the Creme worm we have already discussed. Its impact on the fishing industry deserves further comment. While "rubber" worms have been on the scene for many years, it wasn't until 1949 that the first plastic Creme worm emerged from the mold. That worm started a soft bait transformation in the bass fishing industry that continues to this day. The reason is simple: Plastic worms consistently caught bass and helped anglers win bass tournaments. And due to the ease with which they can be rigged in a

The plastic lizard is an extension of the original plastic worm design.

variety of ways, artificial worms represent very versatile baits. They can be fished, un-weighted, weighted, with scent, as trailers, on the top of the water column, and on the bottom. But then an interesting thing happened on the way to the fishing grounds. East coast saltwater anglers discovered that weakfish loved to eat Mann's Jelly Worms, which were popular as large-mouth bass baits. For a period of time it became a favorite bait for weakfish, even surpassing the use of natural baits for some anglers. Eventually the plastic worm gained greater saltwater acceptance, and has been used effectively for other species of game fish like redfish and striped bass.

As manufacturers of plastic worms become more creative in their worm designs, embedding elements of "smart" designs, other crossover opportunities arise. Salted and scented worms represent baitfish like eels, elvers, and sand launce. Ribbed bodies and undulating tails move water that send signals to the lateral line system of predatory fish. Furthermore, rattles, propellers and other sound-producing features all work to attract fish. New forms of the bait like "wacky worms" and Senko worms have come onto the scene and generated innovative fishing techniques, with applicability in freshwater and saltwater. One of the "pioneer" artificial crossover baits, the plastic worm blazed a trail that is now well-traveled by many contemporary lure designers and manufacturers that produce many other baits that function in much the same manner. Cutting-edge spinner baits, crank baits, stick baits, "jig 'n' pig" combos, and a wide assortment of other hard and soft baits

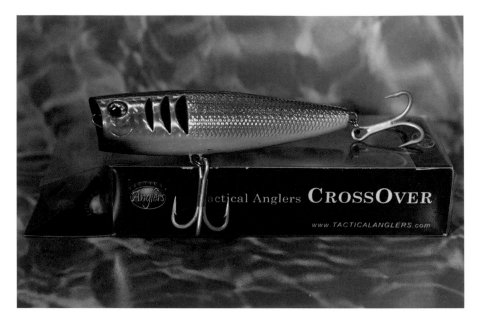

Crossover baits do double duty in both freshwater and saltwater.

have successfully moved between the different mediums of freshwater and saltwater. In some instances anglers have simply modified baits to suit their specific needs. An example of this is changing out the hooks on an artificial freshwater bait to stronger, corrosion-resistant saltwater hooks. Some anglers, especially those who fish salt water, will go so far as to "load" their hard baits. This most often involves drilling holes in a plug and filling the lure with varying amount of water. The water acts as additional balanced weight to enhance casting, and works to affect an element of neutral buoyancy that augments the plug's action.

Along with the use of crossover baits comes application of techniques that also bridge the span between sweet water and the brine. Once again, the "flipping" technique serves as an excellent example. Flipping is a method that was first developed for largemouth bass anglers fishing thickly-matted weed or grass areas or when fishing other forms of tight structure; certain dock and pier configurations qualify in this category. The process of flipping is one that places the angler on a very intimate level with the fish. It is close-quarter angling at its finest. If one proceeds with stealth and if one can find small pods of striped bass around bait-holding structure, the technique is surprisingly effective in salt water. Fundamentally, when flipping,

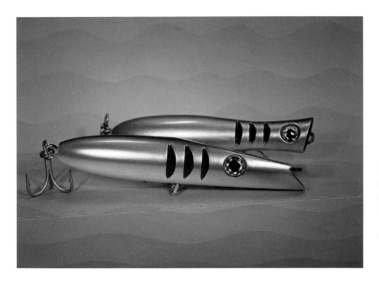

Modifications like recessed gills, oversized eyes, and hollowed-out heads allow water to move around the lure in an enticing way.

the lure is not actually cast but rather delivered to the target location by swinging it in an upward arc and letting it land gently in the water. You can achieve this effect by positioning the rod at a 45-degree angle and stripping approximately four feet of line from the casting reel. Keeping thumb pressure on the reel spool as the rod tip moves quickly toward the water, angle up slightly with wrist motion while simultaneously releasing the spool. Typically, the lure will sink into the zone occupied by fish. As a result, the lure is presented in a vertical fashion—like jigging—rather than moving the lure along a horizontal plane throughout the retrieve. Strikes will occur on the drop or while the lure is moved with a jigging motion. If a fish is in the zone, the hit will often come quickly. With stripers, the take will either be a solid strike, a "bump," or a subtle stop. If the line moves or changes direction, set the hook.

Another similar, up-close technique that works very well for stripers holding in areas like grass banks, multiple dock configurations, and along piers is "pitching." This underhand method is used when you require a short, accurate cast to place a lure in a potential fish-holding zone. It is especially useful when you desire pinpoint placement such as when casting to deep cuts between sections of a sod bank, or even openings in riprap or rock formations. By using a flick-of-the-wrist to cast, the lure travels along a low trajectory, often enabling it to be skipped under obstacles or to access tight spaces. I've had excellent results with this method while slowly drifting close to jetties and rock outcroppings. One memorable success with this technique was a twenty-pound striper that I visually pitched to as it sat in a sand pothole adjacent to a rocky shoreline. A perfect strike! Boulders situated in shallow- or moderate-depth water also represent good target locations. One of the absolute best places to use this method is where striped bass hang in areas around docks, and actually seek shelter in inaccessible places under the docks. This fishing is much like Florida snook under the dock lights.

Many freshwater bass baits are ideal for crossover applications and will produce excellent results. So, go ahead and add some sweet-water flavor to your saltwater fishing. The results will be rewarding.

CHAPTER 6

THE IMPOSTER QUOTIENT

While it is somewhat cliché, imitation is often the sincerest form of flattery. And for an artificial bait, the paramount form of flattery is that moment when a fish mistakes the imposter bait as a replica of a real food source. The ability to fool a predatory animal such as a fish and getting it to gobble up a piece of plastic, wood, metal, or an amalgamation of feathers is the epitome of imitation. The degree to which a lure is capable of consistently achieving this end result is a function of its Imposter Quotient.

As we have already discussed, there is no question that modern artificial lures are engineered with sound science as a fundamental design element. To understand how contemporary hard and soft baits function, one needs to also understand how they have undergone the transition from being somewhat passive baits that are brought to life by the interaction of the angler, to active baits that in many instances can stimulate fish to feed. I refer to that class of artificial lures as Hi-IQ Baits, where IQ in this instance represents the Imposter Quotient. In the world of human learning the measure of one's brain power is also expressed as IQ, or the Intelligence Quotient. According to various dictionary sources human intelligence is defined as the ability to understand and comprehend, and it is furthermore a combination of reasoning, judgment, imagination, and memory. In essence, intelligence is mix of cognitive skills and acquired knowledge that affects human decisions, problem solving, and overall behavior. But in the world of artificial baits the Imposter Quotient is the measure of a lure's ability to create a realistic impression of a natural bait.

Although fish rely mostly on their sensory networks to navigate their world and live their day-to-day lives, they are also somewhat "intelligent" creatures that demonstrate the ability to learn. While there exists a body of scientific research to support the concept of fish intelligence, there is also significant anecdotal evidence that highlights the ability of fish to learn. I

Creating the illusion of a vulnerable bait leads to success.

have had a number of personal interactions with fish that highlight how they relate to their environments. Whether a function of innate intelligence, conditioned behavior, or learned experiences, fish can be quite adaptive. I have had a number of occasions to witness this firsthand. In one instance, trout kept in hatchery pools can learn to readily distinguish the shape of a human that has been feeding. I've watched hatchery personnel approach a feeding station and as they raise their hands the trout begin to amass and roil the surface, as if they were in the midst of a massive mayfly hatch. This is an example of a conditioned response that produces a learned pattern of behavior. I had a similar experience with an Oscar that I kept in a tank along with a few other tropical fish. That Oscar had learned to distinguish my body shape and profile from among others. When someone would enter the room with me where the tank was located that fish would follow my movements and, for the most part, ignore the other person. I am sure this behavior was attributed to the fact that I was the one who fed the fish. Yet it demonstrated that fish's ability to differentiate between objects. The fish would also become excited when the light in the room was turned on. Furthermore, I eventually got that Oscar to eat directly from my fingers. After he became accustomed to that, he would eagerly rise from the bottom of the tank to the surface whenever he saw me approach the tank with the food canister, another example of adaptive behavior.

Within the realm of wild fish and fishing, a number of carp encounters that I've had work to reinforce the concept of how fish learn. There's a small pond close to where I live that supports a robust population of common carp. The pond also hosts many species of waterfowl that people feed regularly. While I have caught many carp from that pond on a variety of natural and artificial baits, the most consistently-effective baits have been those that imitate the food fed to resident and transient waterfowl. The reason is that the local carp became accustomed to the duck food as "easy-pickings," supplements to their normal diet of natural food. Those carp in particular enjoyed the corn that had escaped the feeding ducks and had sunk to the bottom of the pond. The carp had also become conditioned to prowl the area soon after the flapping and quacking ducks had ceased feeding. Over time, many of the carp in that pond benefitted from the duck feedings and as a result, developed a fondness for food sources like corn. That pattern of behavior offered some interesting angling opportunities.

My fishing experiences for carp in that pond were primarily visual, where I would sight-cast to feeding fish. When not using scented soft plastics or flies, corn was always my bait of choice. Many of the pond's carp would readily eat a well-placed cluster of corn on a hook. One of the benefits of sight casting is that the angler can watch the entire drama unfold. You are able to watch the fish, track its approach, see the take as it feeds, and witness any

Under the right conditions, carp will eat flies tied to match their food sources.

While far from being a purist pursuit, feeding corn and bread flies to carp can be quite productive in duck ponds. Modern materials allow for some creative innovations.

rejections of the bait. So it was with one particular carp that I had caught on a corn bait. This fish had a few unique markings on its jaw that made it very recognizable when it fed in shallow water. I had caught and released the fish one summer and saw it many other times with no real opportunities to present a bait. But later that year, during late fall, the fish cycled back to the area where I had initially caught it and presented me with another casting opportunity. I watch the carp move slowly about and headed in my direction. The fish was churning up the bottom, "mudding" in an attempt to dislodge or roust something to eat. Eventually it came to within casting distance and I placed the corn bait ahead of its path. The fish saw the bait circle it, appeared to smell it and then took off like a bat flying out from the underworld. It was indeed spooked by the corn bait it had once before eaten. I suspect that fish associated the scent of corn with the experience of being caught.

The same scenario unfolded other times with other fish. Was it perhaps an exposed hook that spooked those fish, or a recollection of a past negative event resulting in it being caught? Regardless, I believe those sorts of reactions are an indication that carp have the capacity to learn. By all measures of fish intelligence, carp are reasonably smart creatures. It appears that they have an ability to recall positive and negative experiences, put the pieces together, and react accordingly. In addition to the corn incidents, I have also had a number of other small pond situations where carp would aggressively take a fly or artificial on one trip, and then on subsequent outings to the same area, totally reject those same baits. The refusals were so emphatic it seemed the carp knew the deceptive bait represented something to be avoided. Could it have been a fish that had been previously caught or did that fish's pack mates learn from the negative experience of their buddy? I believe both those scenarios come into play. Similar experiences of other anglers also support this conclusion. It is believed by some anglers that once a carp experiences being caught, that specific fish becomes more difficult to catch again. Is it presumed that memory plays a role in that, whereby it may associate a hook or a bait with the negative experience of being caught.

Psychologists refer to this as associative behavior, and it has also been evident in the behaviors of other species of fish. For example, some fish have been shown to remember colors, while others remember sounds, voices, and various stimulating signals. Perhaps, those stimuli either activate some sensory response or tap into memory and learned behaviors. While this hypothesis is supported primarily by anecdotal evidence derived from the observations of fishermen, the scientific process has also yielded similar conclusions. For example, fundamental science has supported the fact that some species of fish, like the carp, do indeed demonstrate a capacity for memory. One of the unknowns is how long a fish can remember a certain incident or an unpleasant experience. I talked with a veterinarian who indicated that there are some documented experiences with wolves demonstrating an ability to know that one of their pack mates is missing, but that after a period of time they not only forget the episode, but also forget their pack mate. Those memory traits may also be present in certain fish. People have conditioned other fish like catfish, goldfish, and even trout to respond to certain situations. Some species of fish have also demonstrated an ability to use tools to assist in the process of feeding and mating. This indicates some level of problem-solving behavior, a factor used to assess and measure intelligence. Fish can also be socially cooperative creatures, most specifically when engaged in feeding behaviors. One example is sailfish using their sails and each other in concert to push and corral baitfish to the surface of the water. Sailfish also change body colors when homing in on prey. This serves to confuse baitfish and to visually communicate with other sailfish during the hunt.

Carp can be very selective and wary, and exhibit recall. Spooking one from this pack would spook them all.

What does all this have to do with fishing and more specifically, artificial lures? Contemporary smart baits are designed to appeal to how fish sense their world, especially those traits that involve instinct and learned behaviors. A lure in any form is fundamentally a charlatan, a counterfeit of reality that imitates either a singular species or a class of bait. And in some instances a lure replicates nothing natural, but it has all the right stuff to get the attention of fish. The higher the Imposter Quotient of the artificial bait, the more likely it will motivate a response from fish. Whether that bait is hard or soft, new-age lure designers apply significant elements of science and product testing to produce an end result that gets fish stimulated to strike, eat, and aggressively grab on to a lure. This is all good news for anglers, but an understanding of the principles of lure engineering can actually help increase catch ratios. So how do lures accomplish this?

Fish will strike an artificial bait for any number of reasons. And in some instances it will be more than one triggering effect that act as strike stimuli. First and foremost, fish will respond to a lure out of a need to feed. Fulfilling this most basic life necessity is what gets the majority of fish caught. An imposter bait that is capable of appealing to a fish's feeding instincts or learned behaviors will generate more looks and more strikes. In addition to triggering feeding responses, high "IQ" artificial baits can also elicit strikes that appeal to territorial instincts during breeding, as well as curiosity. A smart lure can activate the sensory network of fish and generate a number of responses that ultimately result in a strike. Design characteristics that affect a lure's motion, action, scent properties, shape, size, color, or sound all influence the way in which a fish responds to that bait.

Let's take a look at how intelligent baits accomplish this. Most predatory fish are opportunistic feeders and use a combination of instincts and learned behaviors to feed and survive. A fish's awareness of scent is often the first of its senses to detect the presence of prey. This is especially true in salt water where rafts of bait move about in large masses, emitting intense scent. At times the intensity can be so overpowering that even humans above water can smell the bait, as frequently occurs with masses of menhaden or bunker

High impostor quotients can lead to greater angler success.

that produce a scent very reminiscent of ripe melon. But beneath the water a bait concentration such as that releases high levels of scent into the water. Often combined with released chemical pheromones, this scent disperses for long distances in water and provides the initial clue for predatory fish as to the whereabouts of prey. Chum slicks like those used by shark anglers provide further indication for how this works. As a chum slick builds it creates a scent trail that extends from the boat outward in the direction of the drift. Depending on how much chum is present, a slick can extend for miles. Sharks will very often key in on the end of the slick and work their way back to the origins of the scent. Anglers typically set out natural baits at varying depths in a portion of the slick closest to the boat, hoping the sharks will intercept the baits and eat. But aggressive sharks that come directly to the source of the chum will often rise near the surface where artificial baits, like scented flies, can be presented to them. In addition to the use of scent, savvy shark anglers will use devices that emit sound or electrical impulses to further stimulate the other shark senses. Other highly-predatory fish species will also behave in much the same way. And this behavior is not limited to saltwater fish. In large freshwater impoundments where largemouth bass or landlocked striped bass are present, those species will school up during certain times of the year. Baitfish such as threadfin shad will also be active at these times, and their mass congregations will throw off inviting scents and vibrations that appeal to the lateral lines of bass.

Whether in salt water or fresh water, there is a progression of sensory utilization that most fish depend upon when homing in on a food source, and this approach has significance in the way smart baits are designed and fished. As suggested, it is often the sense of smell that first makes fish aware of baitfish. Subsequently, any vibrations that those baitfish generate will help the predator fish refine the direction and distance of their potential prey. As the fish move closer to the bait, their senses of both smell and sound become fully engaged. Once in the "red zone," visual acuity takes over during the end game. It is a fish's sight that, in essence, closes the deal and enables it to catch its prey. Artificial lures that reproduce the sensory effects of those hunting traits are the ones that have built-in intelligence and work best to promote strikes. Some lures appeal to just one of those triggers, while more sophisticated baits target multiple senses. An example of the former are simple soft plastic baits that have been infused with scent. Many anglers who fish for bottom-dwelling species like summer flounder or fluke will regularly use a bait like this with remarkable success, at times with better results than natural bait. At the opposite end of the spectrum are hard plastic, swim baits with ball bearing rattles, holographic paint, bait-matching sizes and profiles, multiple joints for maximum action when retrieved, and weight-balancing for longer casts and ideal sink rates, to keep the lure in the fish zone for an extended period of time.

Any smart bait with a high Imposter Quotient will have influence upon most if not all of a fish's senses and will appeal to those senses in a manner that is consistent with the way in which fish hunt prey and feed. An equally-smart angler will home in on those senses with an appropriate choice of baits that appear alive or susceptible to predation, give off scent, make noise, present a visually appealing profile, and offer what appears to be an easy meal. The more stimuli an angler puts into action, the better are the chances for a consistent rate of hook-ups. But as effective as contemporary plastic baits may be, the key variable in the equation is the angler, acting to exert influence on the line and lure to make it behave in a natural and realistic way. The sophistication of smart baits give the angler a major advantage over the fish species they target. The baits can work in concert with one's fishing skills to dramatically increase the consistency of the catch.

CHAPTER 7

FLIES AND TEASERS

Hard and soft smart baits are not the only artificial lures to benefit from new-age technology. Flies and teasers both have evolved to the point where sophisticated tying techniques, innovative materials, and creative designs have resulted in a broad spectrum of effective offerings for a wide variety of fish species in saltwater and freshwater. Fly tiers can tie, spin, glue, and wrap feathers, fur, hair, and synthetic materials upon hooks to create a virtually unlimited array of artificial flies. The tying and construction of flies has come a long way since the first enterprising angler wrapped fur and feathers about a hook.

One of the earliest documented accounts of artificial flies being used for fishing can be traced back almost two thousand years to the River Astræus in Macedonia, and the use of an artificial fly to catch "fish with speckled skins." In his book, *The Fly: A History of Fly Fishing*, Dr. Andrew N. Herd references this intriguing Macedonian fly. While there is much scholarly debate as to the actually dressing of that fly, there tends to be agreement as to how and with what materials it was tied. Dr. Herd suggests a possible dressing for this fly and attributes the recipe to William Radcliffe's *Fishing from the Earliest Times* (1921). According to that recipe, Macedonian fly tyers would "fasten crimson red wool around a hook, and fix onto the wool two feathers which grow under a cock's wattle, and which in colour are like wax." As fascinating as his research findings are on the Macedonian fly, Dr. Herd's conclusions regarding saltwater fly fishing are equally intriguing. According to Dr. Herd, "There is a great deal of dispute about who dipped the first fly in the sea, but it happened as least two thousand years ago." His evidence for this belief comes from the writings of Ælian (170–230 AD) of Praeneste, modern-day Palestrina, Italy. Ælian wrote of subjects of natural history and in one of his writings he describes a fishing event: "One of the crew sitting at the stern lets down on either side of the ship lines with hooks.

On each hook he ties a bait wrapped in wool of Laconian red, and to each hook attaches the feather of a seamew [seagull]." While that rendition may not describe the act of fly fishing as we know it today, and for all we know that "wrapped bait" may very well have been the predecessor to the bucktail jig, it does coincide with the timing and of use of the Macedonian fly. And the combination of red wool and the feathers of a European gull do conjure up images of a fly-like lure. Regardless of the fishing method, this process of attaching natural materials onto a hook to fool saltwater fish may very well have been the first building block upon which the foundation of modern fly tying has been built.

The origins of modern fly tying and fly fishing are well rooted in European tradition and the New World imported these practice with colonization. English angling traditions were brought to the colonies with the earliest of settlers, some of whom caught trout and sea-run "salters" on flies along the north Atlantic coast. While trout and salmon were most often the targets of those initial fly anglers, some intrepid pioneers dabbled with flies in saltwater. And some of the earliest accounts of fly fishing in the United States reveal catches of shad and striped bass in the mid-nineteenth century. Evidence also exists that the use of primitive "flies" can be traced back to aboriginal inhabitants of planet earth. These native ancestors were quite enterprising in their use of bone, fur, and feathers to lure fish onto their archaic hooks or into range of their spears. But their efforts were successful and they were able to supplement their diet with fish.

Now let's fast forward to modern era of fly fishing and the influences of technology on the materials used to craft contemporary fly patterns. I once belonged to a fly-tying guild on Long Island, New York and each meeting of the group would always begin in the same fashion. The membership of this organization loved to tie flies; it also believed in sharing information and passing on the skills and traditions of fly tying. This information exchange was never more robust than when it related to the acquisition of materials from non-typical sources. It was sort of a show-and-tell with a "can you top this find?" atmosphere. Before the meeting would officially begin and the tying commenced, it was not unusual to hear a member say, "Hey, look at what I found in the local craft store!" Another might add, "Get a load of this new body material I picked up in the hardware store!" Yet another would offer, "How about this flash? Found it in a supermarket over by frozen foods!"

Frozen foods? You never know where the next great tying discovery will be made. One of today's most productive trout flies utilizes a material found mixed in with car cleaning soaps and waxes. It is quite rewarding to make a find of this sort or to simply be guided in the direction of a new source of tying materials. Fly tying is as much about the journey of discovery as it is about the final destination of producing a hand-crafted fly and catching a fish with it. Today's era of fly-tying is most intriguing. When it comes to materials availability, quality, and diversity, a boundless wealth of possibilities lay before us as a result of technology and its influence on the market place. The really creative and innovative fly tiers constantly push the edge of the envelope and experiment with all sorts of atypical materials. You can't always guess the fish appeal of a new element on a fly. Fish are the ultimate deciders.

Traditions of classic fly fishing aside, the world of fly tying is a now a wide-open game and innovation is evident in both saltwater and freshwater fly tying. Just like with hard and soft artificial baits, realism in fly tying is taking hold over impressionism. Just about anything goes if it results in a realistic fly that fish are willing to eat. I've talked with many fly tiers about their willingness to go beyond what was once considered the normal and acceptable boundaries of fly tying to embrace materials and techniques that add an entirely new edge to modern fly patterns. One such tier is Long Island's Glenn Mikkleson. He exemplifies the creative curiosity that all tyers have who push edge of the envelope. While very capable of tying classic fly patterns, Glenn is by far an exceptional fly innovator in the world of saltwater fly fishing. His patterns are inventive, durable, highly effective, and artfully crafted. Glenn's views on modern fly tying, especially regarding the use of modern adhesives, synthetics, and super glues add a unique perspective to any fly tier who strives to think outside the box:

> The old traditions of fly tying had these unwritten rules that forbade the fly tier from "cheating" by using non-traditional methods. If they did, their product was not considered a fly, and if used to catch a fish, well, that really wasn't fly fishing; they were even considered non-ethical anglers. This is the ridicule anglers faced at one time if they decided to fish a wet fly instead of a dry fly. Salmon fly tying and fishing are loaded with do's and don'ts

regarding methods and procedures, tactics and conduct. All had their reasons, though some are now antiquated. When I started tying, it seemed the use of most adhesives was frowned upon by the purists. They tended to shun most introductions of synthetics to their craft. This attitude tended to stifle experimentation. As new people flooded the sport, the old traditions and the rules that accompanied them were forgotten or ignored. This opened the door to accelerated innovation and expanding the boundaries of what was considered a fly. Nowadays modern adhesives and synthetics are the sole ingredients of some popular patterns. Although I still prefer natural hairs and feathers to the synthetics for most of my patterns, I do utilize the variety of glues that the traditionalists didn't have available to them forty years ago.

Once upon a time I knew a very talented young fly tier. His work was excellent and he would strive to constantly improve his tying. Whenever he tied a new design he would ask my opinion. I'd always smile and respond: "Looks good, but you are not trying to catch me." Regardless of how appealing or attractive a fly might look out of the water, or how well it is tied, the fish are both judge and jury. In the final analysis a fly, like other effective artificial

Epoxy flies are durable and effective.

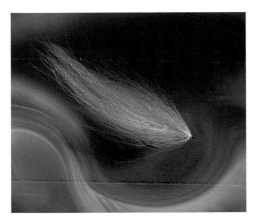

The Popovics Bucktail Deceiver and The Beast are examples of new-age flies that replicate large prey baitfish.

baits, must appear real to a fish and also appeal its feeding instincts. Flies with high Imposter Quotients get the most attention. To that point, Mikkleson has suggested that both balance and symmetry are very important in the construction of flies if a realistic presentation is to be made. "Most often, flies have to swim right to get hits. Keep your flies balanced and symmetrical. Put the bulk of more buoyant materials above the ballast weight of the hook bend to ensure your pattern will ride upright.

"Adding weight can change everything, so test a new design before you tie up a dozen–it just might need adjustments. With all the effort and expense we have invested in our sport, it doesn't make sense to offer the fish flies that don't perform as well as they could. The fly should be the only bit of tackle the quarry sees and quite often is the one that is most responsible for our success."

TEMPT, TANTALIZE, AND TEASE

What's in a name? That which we call a rose
by any other name would smell as sweet.
—William Shakespeare, *Romeo and Juliet*

A "teaser" is in all design respects very much a fly, but it is not usually fished with fly gear. Teasers are adjuncts to conventional terminal tackle and used most often for bottom species such as summer flounder, sea bass, striped bass, weakfish, and cod. They are designed to tempt, tantalize and "tease."

Teasers add appeal to a lure or a terminal rig.

Essentially, there is little conceptual difference between flies and teasers. The key for effectiveness with either lies in the design and the principle of the three S's: shape, silhouette, and size. Teasers and flies are also most often tied with tails, bodies, bellies, and top wings, among other subtle touches. Add in contrasting colors for good measure and you have the right formula for success, whether for use as a fly or a teaser. When crafting teasers, as with any good fly design, the end product should be durable, easy to tie, and as foul resistant as possible.

The primary objective of using a fly or teaser is to create the illusion of a life form that is vulnerable to predation by game fish; it needs to look good enough to eat. In the case of a fly, that deception is achieved through the specific design of the pattern and the way it is retrieved. A teaser most often draws its strikes by being a part of a tandem rig and works in concert with another artificial bait. When paired with a plug, the impression is given of a small fish being chased by a larger one; typically a reaction strike is the result. Yet, there are also times, much like with a fly, when the teaser alone triggers a strike. What is expected is that a game fish will be attracted to the commotion, put two and two together, and then hit either the teaser or the trailing plug in a moment of competitive urge, hunger, or territorialism. Teasers can also be used as droppers in tandem with bucktails and diamond jigs. Very often the stimulus for a fish to strike a teaser or fly has less to do with anatomical accuracy of the imitation and more to do with the way the artificial is manipulated during the retrieve. Modern teasers are crafted using a wide range of materials, from plain white bucktail to sophisticated synthetic blends. One of the best examples of this trend are the teasers tied by Long Island's Harvey Cooper using a combination of modern synthetic materials blended by Captain Ian Devlin, who hails from Connecticut. Devlin's "Devil N Blend" is a unique mix of synthetics of varying colors that include single tones, a 3D Blend, and a Super Blend. Through the merging of materials and colors, a blend of this nature is capable of delivering more realistic and life-like movement and coloration that mimics the attributes of natural baitfish. Cooper's teasers have enticed and caught a wide range of fish species including striped bass, bluefish, weakfish, fluke, blackfish, sea bass, scup, cod,

Fly tiers can craft teasers in very realistic fashion.

and other bottom feeders. His teasers are a staple in the tackle boxes of many boat and surf anglers. Harvey talks enthusiastically and passionately about his masterfully-tied creations, but never in the context of his teasers being flies. He will readily tell you that he is neither a fly tier nor a fly fisherman, but rather views the results of his tying as simply "teasers." Yet, his work, especially his bunker and epoxy patterns, are as much at home tied to the ends of fly leaders as they are tied ahead of a plug, soft bait, or a hook baited with spearing and squid.

Captain Ian Devlin's development of his synthetic blends began at a Danbury, Connecticut fishing show where renowned angler and fly tier, David Skokie, demonstrated his fiber and flash blending technique. Devlin was intrigued by the concept and was further inspired by the blending methods of New Jersey's noted fly tier Steve Farrar. Devlin experimented with various flash and fiber blends, material stiffness and suppleness, and the effects of blending various colors. He has made literally hundreds of synthetic blends over the years in varying styles and color combinations. Devlin will tell you that the potential of blending is limitless: "It is an endless hole you go down, limited only by your creativity." The use of modern age synthetics and associated tying techniques have added an entirely new dimension to the process of tying flies and teasers. And blends can give the angler an edge when presenting an artificial bait to a fish. According to Devlin, "Blended materials are often more attractive to the fish by the illusion of depth through mixed colors on a fly. You can get a more natural look, or a flashy and highly visible look too. The materials are extremely durable, which is good assurance when you make a nice pattern."

DOUBLE DUTY

Some best fly patterns can easily perform double duty as effective teasers. The reverse of that is also true. Those patterns that trigger a natural response are the most productive. Epoxy flies and teasers are a prime example of this dual functionality. The generic epoxy fly or teaser can be easily modified to match the size and color of prevalent baitfish and the epoxy bodies make them wear extremely well, especially in rocky and sandy locations. One of the best attributes of a well-tied epoxy fly or teaser is that it is very resistant to fouling. Inherent in the construction of an epoxy pattern is that newer underbody materials allow for variations in body color and the addition of built-in flash. Typical tail materials include bucktail, calf tail, foxtail, and an entire range of synthetics. Some tiers will also use short tips of saddle hackle. The challenge is to use materials subtle enough to allow for seductive action, yet stiff enough to minimize fouling.

One of the oldest and most effective fly designs that can be converted to use as a teaser is the simple hairwing pattern. One of the very best is exemplified by the Joe Brooks' Blonde series of flies that originated in the 1950s and is still going strong today in its original form and in numerous variations. Brooks developed the Blonde initially for use on freshwater trout, salmon, and black bass. It was one of the earliest hair flies to be used in saltwater fly fishing, and it makes a great teaser. Such flies often employ Bucktail as a hairwing tail and then single or double clumps of hair attached on the topside of the hook shank as a wing. Flash is wrapped along the hook shank to provide additional spice. What I like about hairwing patterns for teasers is that they are easier to tie than most other flies, and that they are foul resistant. Additionally, bucktail can be dyed in such a wide array of colors, that it makes matching local bait hues and tones a relatively easy task. A splendid variation of the hairwing that is quite effective as a teaser

Simple and effective, the Brooks Blonde pattern can vary with the use of modern materials.

is the "Hi-Tie," a design whereby multiple hair wings are affixed to the topside of the hook shank. The extra sets of wings give additional body bulk to the fly's profile.

But all bucktail is not created equal. For saltwater use, try to find the largest fibers possible. And remember that not all the fibers of a tail are suitable for a fly or a teaser. The finer, longer strands of hair work the best. Unless you want to create a very splayed or wide-profile teaser, stay away from the larger-diameter hairs. Other materials suitable for use when tying teasers include but are not limited to natural and synthetic materials, such as fox hair, elk hair, Icelandic sheep, EP Fibers (Enrico Puglisi), Angel Hair, Yak Hair, Bozo Hair, Devil N Blend, Slinky Fiber, and FishHair.

EASY BODIES AND MODERN SYNTHETICS

There are a number synthetic materials on the market that enable the tier to craft creative flies and teasers. EZ-Body is an example of one such material, as are Mylar tubing, Flexi-Cord tubing, Corsair tubing, and Holographic tubing. The tube material can be placed either on the hook shank or placed over an underbody material to give shape and consistency to the design and present a more lifelike form. Foam is another such material since it acts as floatation and enables the teaser to flutter about like a wounded baitfish. A teaser of this nature can be very simple to construct. It requires an appropriate length of tubing, consistent with the size and shape of the bait to be matched, to be threaded onto a hook and shaped to the desired form. A simple tail, affixed eyes, and a whip-finished head complete the fly. If one chooses to tie a somewhat more complex teaser of this design, you can add a wing, very often with a rabbit fur strip for additional attractiveness. But with easy-body types of teasers, simpler is better. When using easy body materials for flies the simplest designs can be amazingly effective. One of the advantages of tubing is that is enables you to easily shape the streamlined body style of most local baitfish—whether they are sand eels, silverside, or anchovies. The tubing also comes in a number of different textures and color finishes such as pearl, silver, holographic, and clear. Strips of holographic or 3D flash enhance appeal. When finishing the teaser it is advisable to coat it with a layer of Hard as Nails clear nail polish or some other similar hardening agent. This not only makes the fly or teaser more durable, but the transparent shine adds an appealing flash.

Materials were never more abundant than they are in today's market.

MANY CHOICES

Numerous flies can work as teasers, some of which might never be associated with that application. The Crease Fly is one such pattern. It is one of the best flies ever created, yet very rarely talked about in terms of teasers.

This genuinely original and world-famous fly was the brainchild of Long Island's Captain Joe Blados. The Crease Fly has taken game fish all across the angling world. It can be tied in quite a number of sizes and color combinations. The idea first hit me to consider this fly as a teaser when I noticed the similarities between the concave popping mouth of my favorite topwater plug and the hollowed-out mouth cavity of the Crease Fly. All I could envision was the chaotic popping and spitting going on all over the surface of the water as bass and bluefish would vie for who got to the ruckus first to tear at the source of the disturbance. The Crease Fly's inherent buoyancy makes it a great choice as a teaser. The fly or teaser is designed to float, aided by the foam underbody, and to create a somewhat of a commotion as it is retrieved. The effect of a Crease Fly teaser being retrieved ahead of a sputtering water-pushing popper is especially effective when tied in the smaller sizes, and fished as a sub-surface pattern.

Numerous other fly designs can also make fine teasers. Another example: A Clouser Minnow with small barbell eyes will sink slightly ahead

A creation of Captain Joe Blados, the Crease Fly is an innovative example of the use of modern materials.

of a pursuing popper and may give the impression of a sounding baitfish. Lefty's Deceivers have been a mainstay of the fly-fishing ranks for many years. Tie them slim and in attracting colors and they work exceptionally well as teasers, as do squid flies, hair-bug flies, eel flies, sliders, and popping bugs.

CREATIVE ADDITIVES

There are no steadfast rules to follow when tying teasers and flies. Other than learning the fundamentals of tying flies, allow your imagination to take you down a creative path and let the fish tell you which "ties" they like. To that end, modern fly tiers embrace all forms of add-ons that can make a pattern more attractive to fish. While some may view it as heresy to tie against the purity of fly fishing's dry-fly roots, adding non-traditional components to a fly can often make the design appeal to multiple senses and, therefore more tempting to fish. In essence, this creates a smarter fly. Additives include elements like imbedded rattles, small spinner blades, scent pockets, and balanced weight. Modern tiers will even incorporate tying devices like articulation and and the addition of silicone diving lips on flies to impart more realistic motion and action when retrieving the fly. The inspiration for this creativity is often prompted by the challenges that anglers face from either difficult fishing conditions or the selective feeding habits of demanding fish species. Those are the conditions that advance the art of fly tying and lead to smarter and more technically superior flies and teasers.

CHAPTER 8

WHAT'S THAT SMELL?

When my daughter was young she would not eat anything without first smelling it. To her way of thinking at the time, she could not consume any food unless it first passed her own sniff test. If it smelled good then all was well and down the gullet it would go. But if the food had any sort of unappealing or unknown odor she would hold out the piece of food on her fork for all the world to see and ask, "What's that smell?" But even with most adults, that is a pretty standard practice before we engage in eating some new or foreign foodstuff.

While alluring aromas convey positive signals to the human palate, smell is a very important sense in guiding predatory fish to their prey. A good example of this can be seen in saltwater when Atlantic menhaden, or bunker, amass in large numbers in harbors and bays. Their concentrations are often so dense that they will emit a melon-like aroma that is detectable by humans. But what is even more noteworthy is that the odors released into the water by bunker can travel great distances and act as natural attractants for predators. Most often it is a fish's sense of smell that makes it initially aware of prey, and it is that scent which provides general directional influence as to where those fish should head for their next meal. Once scent has allowed a fish to get in the right zone where prey bait is present, it is usually the sense of hearing that guides them further toward their objective. In the case of bunker, they will typically splash leisurely about the surface of the water in calm fashion when not being harassed by larger fish intent on eating them. These movements generate sounds that interact with the lateral lines of pursuing fish. When the menhaden feed and interact socially they also release pheromones that allow them to communicate with their school mates, and that activity can further work to guide the predators closer. Once fish like striped bass and bluefish zero in on the bunker, their eyesight takes hold during the final phase of the hunt. Although these fish now become sight predators, it was scent that acted as the first-phase stimulus for feeding.

Moldable scents are efficient for many species of game fish.

It has been known for a long time by bait fishermen that "smelly" baits are exceptionally effective for catfish and carp, since both species rely heavily on their sense of smell to feed. In salt water, chumming for bluefish and sharks also has the same positive effects since those species slso depend on scent signals to track down their prey. And for years, anglers have tried to enhance the allure of their artificial baits by adding various scents and potions to entice fish to strike. I recall many freshwater bass anglers who would soak their plastic worms in anise solutions back when those artificial baits were first introduced. The result of that technique yielded positive results. While it was not known if additives like anise and licorice simply masked residual human scent or actually attracted fish, those sorts of adjuncts, anecdotally, did indeed motivate bites. And anglers being the curious and innovative lot that they are, continued to experiment with homemade enhancement to their baits.

A number of years ago new products came onto the market and in several respects changed the way many anglers fish. These products were developed with a substantial amount of science at their core. One such revolutionary product, Gulp! was developed by the Berkley company. This soft, pliable bait is constructed using water-based resins that allow scent to be readily and intensely dispersed into the water. This hallmark characteristic has shown to be extremely effective in its ability to attract fish to a bait via released scent, and to then cause those fish to eat the bait. This has been proven for both freshwater and saltwater species. In some fishing circles the use of Gulp! baits has even surpassed prior utilization of live bait. On Long Island, where I fish, it has become standard operating procedure to use scented baits like Gulp! for many bottom-dwelling species of fish like fluke, or summer flounder. It also works well for other species like scup and sea bass. In many instances this "smart" artificial actually outperforms natural bait. I have had many personal experiences using this form of artificial as a teaser and scored more hits than the natural bait that was suspended below it. The other significant attribute of this genre of pliable soft baits is that they can match the size, shape, and profile of the natural bait that they imitate. The specific scent of prey species can then be infused into the bait giving it a multi-dimensional appeal. So when a fish encounters this type of soft bait it is a package that can not only attract the interest of fish, but also prompt a response that more than likely will result in a strike. The science behind these innovative baits has undergone the rigors of both laboratory and field testing. Scientists toil over various chemical formulas to achieve the best possible replication of natural scents.

From an angler's perspective, scent is an important weapon in one's tackle arsenal, but not all fish are created equal with respect to how they respond to diffused odors that come into their environments. Fish species that root about the bottom of a lake or stream like catfish, or saltwater species that feed along the ocean bed, will often rely heavily on their sense of smell, as will fish that live in typically murky and rivers with roiled water. To the extent that these conditions hamper other senses or methods of finding prey, scent—through a network chemoreceptors—will play a large role in a fish's foraging behaviors. Understanding these interactions will be determining factors in an angler's success. Peter Cowin is the founder and president of BioEdge Fishing Products, established in 2007. Since that time, Cowin's company has been involved in the business of producing an array of scents and potions for use in fishing. BioEdge creates scents from all-natural ingredients containing oils, amino acids, pheromones, and proprietary feeding stimulants in two forms of scented products: Liquid potions and glue-like stick wands. Anglers can apply both of these scented offerings to hard and soft baits, rather than being infused into the baits, such as the Gulp!-like products, and both are effective on either form of artificial lure. Personally, I prefer the glue-stick application for hard baits and the liquid potions for soft plastic baits, since I feel that approach enhances the effectiveness of the scent on those different types of materials.

Although some purists may consider it heretical, scent applied to flies can be effective as well. With today's high-tech synthetics, acrylics, binding agents, rattles, and so on, flies have come a very long way from their purist origins. In classic angling tradition, dry flies replicated a variety of aquatic and terrestrial insects that floated in the surface film. For insects like may flies, stone flies, and caddis flies, the artificial dry fly represents the stage of the insect's life where it either emerges from the water column to float in the current before flying off, or when it spins or falls back to the water at the end of its life cycle. At one point, the dry fly was the epitome of fly fishing. But over time, anglers embraced streamer flies that imitated baitfish, and both wet flies and nymphs that mimicked sub-surface stages of insect's life. That liberalization eventually allowed for open-ended innovation with the creation of new patterns and an entirely new perspective on what constitutes a fly. Times have indeed changed and it is now no-holds-barred when it comes to what a fly is or isn't. An extension of that contemporary mindset is the addition of scent to flies.

One of the best examples of this is when fly fishing for apex predators like sharks. One specific experience highlights the effectiveness of pairing both feathers and scent. Some friends and I were drifting amidst a chum slick twenty miles off the south shore of Long Island. My goal was to get a mako shark up into the slick, close enough to tempt it to eat a fly. Since that wait-and-see fly game can be tedious to some, my fishing companions decided break with boredom and place traditional baits out at varying depths of thirty, sixty, and ninety feet. That would dramatically decrease my odds for getting a shark in the slick, since natural baits like bluefish, false albacore, and menhaden would typically always get a shark's attention first, and they would, therefore, be more likely to eat one of those baits. It was a slow day with very little activity, but late afternoon brought with it the visual of a fin breaking the surface of the water about a hundred yards from the boat. The shark moved toward the farthest bait and circled the float to which the bait was attached. I was sure it was going to eat, but it didn't. The shark then proceeded to approach the remaining two baits. It circled them but then again didn't eat. As the shark left the closer of those two baits I could see that it was on track to move up the slick and toward the boat. I readied my rod and for good measure doused the fly in some rather smelly bunker oil. The small mako moved within casting range and I cast the fly in a manner that it drifted in the slick with pieces of chum. The mako swam toward the fly and then turned away, only to turn back around. It tracked right to the fly and ate it. I landed the mako on the fly rod and eventually released it. The mystery was why that fish had refused the various natural baits that were easy pickings to ultimately eat a mass of feathers that had been scented with bunker oil. Needless to say, my fellow anglers were as intrigued as I. Following that trip I also experienced similar situations with blue sharks that passed up easy meals to grab a scented fly. One such fish materialized from the depths around the boat to snatch my offering from among a buffet of baits. These situations got me to thinking about the reasons why this feeding behavior occurred. After much contemplation and talking with other anglers and folks who study shark behavior, I concluded that both the mako and the blue shark responded to multiple stimuli presented by the fly.

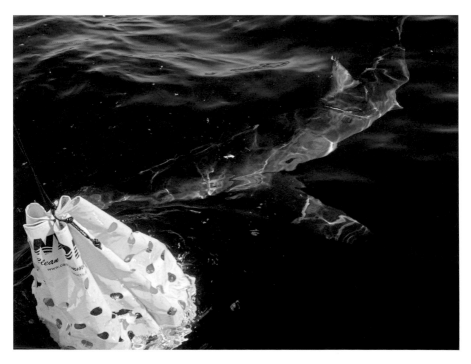

All sharks respond well to dispersed scent.

Those elements were motion, color, and scent. While it still remains somewhat of a mystery why those sharks completely ignored the natural baits, there is a high degree of certainty that the fly appealed to several senses that, when activated, triggered the strikes. I've since encountered situations where other sharks have either accepted or rejected fly offerings, and one common theme emerges: A liberal dose of scent to the fly always received more attention than scentless flies. It appears that the degree to which the scent or potion elicits a response depends to a large extent upon the intensity of the scent and how well those chemical signals are able to convince a fish that what they are encountering is indeed a real form of food. As I have referenced many times throughout this book, the effectiveness of any artificial bait lies in its capacity to create the deceptive impression that a fraudulent bait is a living creature that can be eaten. The more of an illusion a lure creates, the greater the chances of it being perceived as real. So in that overall equation, scent plays a major role.

Predators like sharks are not the only species to rely heavily on their sense of smell. Certain very prolific freshwater species like catfish and carp also use a highly-developed sense of smell to seek out their food. Under many conditions both species utilize smell and touch as their primary senses for locating a meal. Therefore, many dedicated anglers who fish for both of these species are noted for their dependence on using highly scented baits

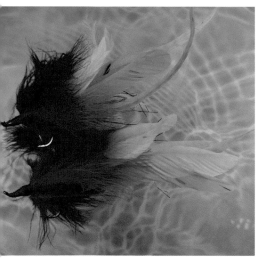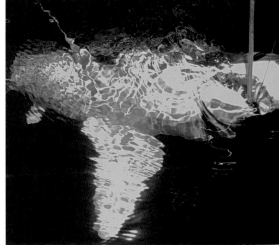

Large, gaudy flies in response-stimulating colors get the attention of aggressive sharks.

with intense odors. In the case of carp anglers, they will often pre-seed an area with scented attractants and then return at a later time to fish baits with similar appeal. This technique can also work in favor of the angler fishing artificial baits. There are two options to consider. The first is to imitate exactly the scent of the food source the fish feed on. For example, if carp in a particular body of water feed heavily on small crustaceans, then the attractant should replicate as precisely as possible the chemistry of that scent. But there is a second alternative to consider: go completely against the grain. That means using scent mixtures that may not replicate the exact food source, but rather have a stimulating effect on a fish's feeding triggers.

Carp anglers are well known for their willingness to experiment with just about any scent or concoction of scents that might yield incremental bites. Peter Cowin of BioEdge Fishing Products sheds some new light on that scenario. According to Peter, there is an interesting development with the use of his scents and potions on the European carp-fishing scene. Some of those carp anglers have discovered that various scents not normally associated with attracting carp have proven effective at triggering reaction bites and stimulating carp to feed. According to Cowin, European carp anglers are using certain BioEdge scents like mackerel and crab with success, although those saltwater species do not appear on these carps' diets. It would appear that both those concentrated scents impact upon chemoreceptors, which activate sensory interest and a feeding response. The major takeaway from this is that it pays for anglers to experiment with different scents, since some of the most unexpected potions might add to the overall effectiveness of any given artificial bait. Cowin further offers that commercial European lobster and crab fishermen are applying various scents to their traps to supplement the appeal of traditional baits.

The design and application of integrated smart baits rely heavily on the principle that the artificial lure generates an impression of life, and that when in use, rouses multiple sensory mechanisms in fish. A bait's "smartness" is directly related to its ability to excite a fish to a point where demonstrates interest in an artificial lure, and then ideally strikes that bait. Scent has a prominent place in that set of circumstances and it is the smart angler who will strive to use that additional tool to his or her advantage.

CHAPTER 9

IT'S ALL ABOUT THOSE BASS

Bass fishing in the United States is as close to being a quasi-religious phenomenon as an outdoor sport can become. It is safe to say that black bass, including both largemouth and smallmouth bass, are one of the most popular and sought-after freshwater game fish in the world. Its legions of followers are dedicated, passionate, and well-organized when it comes to pursuing their favorite quarry. But one of the biggest impacts of the quest for bass has been the innovation and technological advancements that the sport has brought to the recreational fishing scene. As the old maxim suggests: this is not your grandfather's bass fishing.

Like many young and aspiring anglers, my first association with fishing occurred on a small lake. Bluegills and yellow perch kept me busy and ignited the fire that grew through my years on the water. But it was that first largemouth bass that forever changed the game for me. I became obsessed with wanting to catch bass consistently, and then to break new ground into the "lunker" bass category. At the time, my sources for learning about bass were books and the Big Three magazines: *Sports Afield*, *Outdoor Life*, and *Field and Stream*. And every once in a while I'd run into some older bass sharpie who would be willing to share a secret or two and help me up my game. But then, during the late 1960s, Ray Scott, an enterprising visionary, formed the Bass Angler's Sportsman's Society. BASS revolutionized the sport. Founded with the objectives of fostering competitive bass fishing, ethics in angling, and a conservation mindset, BASS established a strong foothold within the fishing community and spawned the growth of club chapters across the United States and the world. In addition to promoting their philosophy of catch-and-release, what caught the attention of the angling public was the concept of organized competitive bass tournaments.

Recreational and tournament anglers are always seeking out the newest innovations in artificial lures. Credit: Greg Kiessling.

Many anglers welcomed the opportunity not only to engage in a contest between themselves and the fish, but also now had the chance to compete against other bass anglers in a test of skill. Local and regional chapter clubs sprung up throughout the United States with tournaments held at each organizational level. The goal of participating anglers was to qualify for inclusion in a particular state tournament that would allow for participation in regional contests, and then compete in the highly-coveted national event, the Bass Master Classic. Winners of the national competition would receive significant prize money, exposure, and product endorsement deals. From this potential emerged a new career path for many anglers, that of professional bass fisherman. Once this happened, the stakes of the game got much higher. Competition against fellow anglers moved the bar to a level never seen before in the recreational fishing industry. Tournament bass anglers now had to demonstrate their acquired skills and knowledge about bass behavior and feeding habits, as well as their ability to catch the highest combined weight of fish during the prescribed tournament time parameters. More often than not, success came in the form choosing and using the right artificial bait to match the fishing conditions and the feeding patterns of bass. To that end, the industry witnessed a period of explosive growth in the design of new and innovative artificial lures. With prize money, prestige, and product endorsements on the line, professional bass anglers sought any edge in the competitions. That advantage was usually the lure tied to the ends of their lines.

For many years the iconic image associated with hooking a lunker largemouth was one of the bass soaring skyward from the water's surface with a classic wooden plug dangling from its jaws. Top-water lures and bass were a match made in heaven. But as any bass angler knows all too well, that marriage of fish and lure works best under certain conditions, as was the case with other popular lures of the time, like in-line spinners, swimming plugs with diving lips, a variety of metal spoons like the vintage Johnson Minnow,

Freshwater bass anglers have a greater array of artificial lures at their disposal than ever before.

and bucktail jigs tipped with pork rind. The old wooden plug and its contemporaries were neither lures for all occasions nor always fitting for the rigors of tournament fishing. Granted, those artificial baits, when used as part of an overall arsenal and strategy, allowed the angler to fish throughout the water column. But the burgeoning demands of the tournament circuit required baits to be much more diverse and suitable for all fishing conditions, as well as any situations anglers encountered on the lake.

Lure manufacturers rose to the occasion and began to produce artificial lures that both challenged the *status quo ante* and, as a result, brought new and exciting baits onto the fishing scene. With the ranks of both recreational and professional tournament bass anglers growing exponentially, lure manufactures had, in essence, a large and readily-available resource with which to test their baits. Feedback was almost instantaneous. If a bait didn't perform in crucial competitive situation, both the bass and the fishermen rejected it. This ultimately brought about a competition amongst lure manufacturers to produce winning artificial baits that could perform when a tournament title was on the line.

This increased need for new and improved tackle box choices was accompanied by a mass desire to learn more about bass habitat, habits, and feeding behaviors. Skills once acquired through learned and intuitive angler experiences were now being supplemented by science and research. A name that immediately comes to my mind is Elwood Buck Perry, a former math and physics high school teacher and college instructor. He was one of the first to apply the rigors of the scientific process to unlock certain secrets of bass fishing. Since fishing with his father from an early age, Perry was fascinated by the concept that bass lived primarily in deep water and traveled on paths from the depths to the shallows. He carried that belief and focused interest with him throughout his life and angling career, and dedicated himself to his own path of discovery about bass behavior. Over time and with many hours of personal research, Perry developed the concept of migratory patterns of bass behavior that guided the fish to and from feeding and resting areas via specific routes. From this intensive study emerged Perry's model of structure fishing. His detailed analysis of how bass would relate to various subsurface configurations and formations like boulders, rocks, submerged trees, substrate, contour, and depth changes was groundbreaking. He even designed and engineered his own hybrid "Spoonplug" that enabled him to fish areas where bass tended to congregate. Although Perry been working on his theories for the better part of three decades, it wasn't until 1979 and the release of his book, *Spoonplugging: Your Guide to Lunker Catches*, that Perry's ideas on structure fishing really took hold.

Perry's concept was so well received that he became known as the "Father of Structure Fishing." Anglers of all skill levels began to embrace structure fishing, because this method gave them the opportunity to catch bass consistently, not just when they were in shallow water. Deep-water structure fishing became the rage, and professional bass anglers took notice. Successful tournament fishing required an angler to be proficient at catching bass at all times of the day and under sometimes adverse conditions. Those conditions often dramatically changed bass feeding patterns and behaviors. But there was an emerging constant that under those conditions, like high pressure systems and cold fronts, bass would often retreat to a comfort zone in deeper water. The trick then became getting them to strike an artificial bait. And that is where the industry began to see changes in lure design and implementation. While bass will always orient toward shallow water structure under favorable conditions, anglers were placing more emphasis throughout the course of a fishing day on finding fish in their deeper water haunts, as well as when those fish were migrating to and from deep water sanctuaries and resting areas. This form of fishing generated an entirely new level of interest in artificial lures that would be effective at lower depths.

One of my first experiences using a swimming lure designed to get down to where the bass were either holding or in transition was with Cotton Cordell's Big O, a then-new diving crankbait design. I had read about the lure in several magazines and purchased a few in the gold color. With most of my bass fishing taking place in shallow ponds and small lakes, I didn't have much opportunity to use the bait until an occasion when I was fishing a local bass tournament with a good friend. The lake we fished was one of the largest bodies of freshwater on Long Island containing a significant amount of deepwater areas. The day's fishing was somewhat slower than we had expected, with only a few largemouth bass apiece. We had been prospecting the shoreline, casting a variety of top-water and shallow-swimming plugs. Having fished this lake previously, we knew of a location where the water dropped off from a weed line. We headed toward that area with my Hummingbird "Bird Trap flasher/finder" showing the way. Approaching the target spot, we saw the telltale signs of the weed bed. We moved farther offshore from it to find the breakline, were the depth increased. As we did, the flashers revealed some marks suspended about five or six feet beneath the boat. We drifted somewhat beyond those marks and made casts back toward he weed line. I had tied on my Big O, in hope that it would ride down the slope and intercept those suspended fish, and that it did. That first cast enticed a smallmouth, as did several subsequent casts. We managed our tournament limit and the Big O yielded enough weight for us to take the top spot in the contest. Over the course of that summer I used that crank bait as much as I could and whenever the opportunity presented itself. It was called into service so much that the gold finish was worn clean, revealing a bone white underbody. I continued to fish the lure in that condition with even better results. It is no wonder that a Big O craze had taken hold within the bass-fishing community, making it one of the hottest crank baits of the time, and motivating other lure manufacturers to follow the design with similar square-billed baits. Although this bait has withstood the test of time, contemporary manufacturing and imaging techniques and improved materials have made this classic even better.

The Big O wasn't the only artificial bait to gain prominence from the bass-fishing revolution that had taken the angling world by storm. Other baits either emerged as new or transformed from an original design into much smarter and more effective designs. For example, the traditional in-line

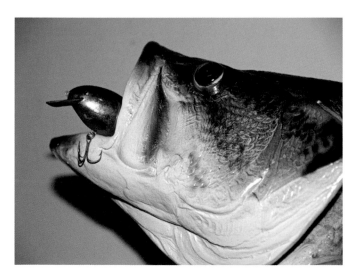

Cotton Cordell's Big O was one of the first of the "alphabet" crank baits.

straight spinner that for decades was a staple of freshwater anglers for all species of fish gave rise to the spinnerbait designed specifically for large-mouth bass. This safety-pin style spinner embraces a design that at first might have you wondering if it could actually catch a fish. But through a unique inter-relationship of shape, weight, balance, and water displacement the spinnerbait is as effective as it is innovative. Additionally, by varying the size, shape, and number of blades installed on the shaft, the lure becomes quite versatile for a number of fishing conditions. Using either single or double blades, and whether those blades are willow-leaf, round, or oblong, will affect the way in which water moves when an angler retrieves the spinnerbait. The throbbing displacement of water generated by that movement results in waves of inviting pulsations that are transmitted through the water and received by a fish's lateral line. Those signals alert bass or other predatory fish that some form of food is in motion and may be struggling as injured prey. The swiftness and aggressiveness with which a spinnerbait is assaulted by bass testifies to its effectiveness. As simple as a spinnerbait may be, it too has benefitted from the age of technology. Modern versions of this bait can

A safety-pin style artificial bait that is as productive as it is versatile.

sport refined paint jobs with realistic features, blades crafted from various metals, and laser-sharpened hooks. The addition of fish-attracting adornments, like fluorescent beads, only add to the bait's appeal. And by varying the head weight, spinnerbaits become versatile lures that can be fished throughout much of the effective water column. This bait became very popular once tournament trail anglers included it in their arsenal of baits and were able to produce winning results. The size, shape, and color of the actual blades used in spinnerbaits can also be modified to match different fishing conditions. In some instances more flash might be desirable, while in other situations, subtler flashing is preferred, Likewise, blade size will determine the amount of water churned during the retrieve and that, at times, can make a difference in getting fish to strike. Color can also play a key role in the effectiveness of spinnerbaits. While gold, copper, and silver blades are most common, painted blades can match a wide spectrum of effective colors.

Other baits that ushered in the new age of bass lures included a variety of plugs, swimbaits, and a wide assortment of soft plastic baits. Traditional plugs and swimbaits have undergone many changes since the relatively primitive days of a lure carved from a chunk of wood. Plastics especially allowed for more innovative designs and overall versatility. One of the more novel enhancements to some modern swim baits is a design feature that allows the bait to remain at specific depths in the water column when the retrieve is halted. This has significant relevance to bass anglers who find fish suspended at those levels in the water column. By using a bait that dives when retrieved and then suspends when the retrieve is halted, an angler can entice more strikes. When that bait is put in motion after being suspended, reaction strikes will often occur. The technology behind this capability is a design and weight-balance that creates an almost neutral buoyancy when the lure comes to a stop. Skilled anglers can actually walk this bait along at desired depths for extended portions of the retrieve. This helps to keep the lure in the "bite zone" for a much longer period of time. While this feature of a lure was born from a need to target suspended freshwater bass, the benefits of suspending baits have reach well into the realm of saltwater fishing. Artificial lures of this smarter genre have caught striped bass, redfish, false albacore, and bluefish, among many other species. This is yet again another example of how innovations targeted for the freshwater bass community have had farther-reaching impacts to much broader fishing communities.

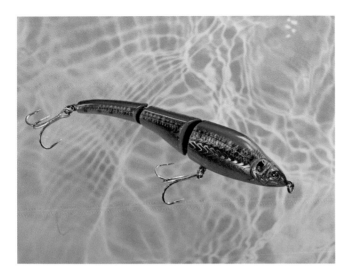

Seductive action is a hallmark of segmented baits.

There is one family of baits that, in my opinion, has had the most profound effect on sport fishing, and that is the family of soft plastic baits. While I have discussed generic plastic baits previously in this book, there is compelling evidence that it was bass fishing which provided the impetus to further innovation of that bait form. The Creme worm was the first significant artificial lure to stimulate major changes in manufacture and use of soft plastic baits. Its impact was felt as early as the late 1940s when the Creme family concocted their first molded worm from a mixture of oils, vinyl, and various colored pigments. The end product resulted in a "worm" that was soft, pliable, and durable, and behaved as if it were alive in the water. By 1951 this synthetic worm was introduced to an eager angling public. While demand for the products grew steadily, it was in the late 1950s when the Creme worm would experience its most significant growth. It was then that bass anglers in the southern Unites States embraced the plastic worm, especially among those anglers who fished in the region's expanding system of impoundments and reservoirs. As the Creme worm gained a reputation as a highly effective bass lures, its popularity grew along with the growth of bass fishing. The folks at Creme recognized this and established a network of bass fishing "field testers" who provided idea and suggestions for product improvement and fishing techniques. The innovations that came about as a result of those interactions not only helped introduce the Creme "Scoundrel" worm to bass anglers but also helped to solidify Creme's position as a company that helped shape an industry. The Creme Lure Company continues to produce not only its signature worm, but an expanded array of other contemporary molded baits.

Not long after molded artificial worms became established as highly-productive baits, other companies emerged to manufacture different forms of molded plastic baits. One of the more popular and effective of those baits was, and still is, the tube lure. A tube lure is simply a hollowed-out segment of soft cylindrical plastic shaped in the form of a tube. The bait is also typically closed at the head and open at the rear, where the plastic is sliced into numerous small strips that resemble tentacles. Given modern pigmentation technology, tube lures are offered in a very broad spectrum of colors. While the original tube lures were initially made with a smooth texture, some later designs featured ribbed bodies. That design causes water to move around the lure and create inviting vibrations detectible by a bass's lateral line. Tube lures were particularly effective for smallmouth bass but embraced by largemouth bass anglers as well. Depending on how the lure is rigged and fished, it could generate significant action, even when the angler does nothing to impart any movement. A tube lure rigged with a weighted jig head will spiral toward the bottom with seductive movement of the plastic tentacles. Bass will often hit this lure on the descent just as a reaction to the inherent movement of the bait. And once on the bottom, a tube lure retrieved slowly and

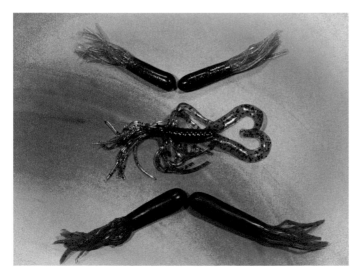

Anglers can rig a tube lure in many ways to handle diverse fishing conditions.

with intermittent pauses and jerks will very much resemble a crawfish or other form of small crustacean.

Tube lures can be rigged in a variety of ways. The most common is with the addition of a jig head or a specially designed weighted head that fits inside the tube, allowing only the tie-in eye to protrude through the top of the lure near the head. Tubes can be fished either as singular baits or with the addition of supplemental adjuncts like plastic tails, plastic grubs, pork rind, as well as various plastic critter and creature-type body forms. One of my most productive tube rigs for smallmouth bass has been a three-inch root beer–colored tube with a half-to-quarter ounce jig head with a similarly tinted twisting-tail grub attached to the hook. Smallmouth have devoured that combination regardless of where I have fish for them. The effectiveness of that tube lure set-up increased in moving water, where bass would hit the bait as it drifted with the current. Very often it only took a slight twitch of the rod tip to motivate any reluctant smallmouth to strike. The "pig 'n' jig" is another lure of this genre that has emerged to handle certain bass fishing conditions. This lure is fundamentally a jig hook that is adorned with either a plastic skirt or natural hair, like bucktail. In its original form, pork rind was then attached as a trailer. This is where the "pig" portion of the name originates.

Over time, bass anglers began to substitute soft plastic baits in lieu of the pork rind. In many instances that trailer would take on the form of a crawfish. Some enterprising anglers would also add rattles into the soft plastic to further mimic the likeness to the sounds made by small crustaceans. Very often this combination worked to create a substantial bait that appeals to larger bass. The generic pig 'n' jig was designed to fish two specific scenarios. The first instance was for flipping and pitching the bait into shallow water cover; an angler essentially lobs the lure into that cover rather than casting it, and works the lure up and down with movements of the rod tip to slowly inch it along. The second method is for use in deep water, where the angler crawls the lure along the bottom in an attempt to simulate a crawfish. Both methods have found favor with both recreational and tournament bass anglers, and with good reason. The pig 'n' jig lure has a proven track record for not only catching big freshwater bass, but for catching numerous bass as well. Tube lures in larger sizes and pigs 'n' jigs have the potential to cross over into saltwater fishing. I have had experiences with both types of lures catching striped bass along docks, bulkheads, and jetties. Fished in similar fashion by casting or pitching into dock structure and then allowing the lures to work along the bottom has produced fine results on saltwater bass. Here we see another example of freshwater bass innovation yielding benefits in the brine. Furthermore, the appeal of plastics on the saltwater scene gave birth to an entirely new family of soft plastic lures known as swim baits. Fabricated to resemble baitfish of all sizes, these artificial baits have a paddle tail that allows them to swim in a very realistic fashion when retrieved.

In the manner that pig 'n' jig lures have captivated the attention of black bass anglers, so too have swim baits grabbed the interest of both freshwater and saltwater anglers alike. These baits are molded from soft plastic and contain keel weights affixed to a hook rigged through the body of lure. This allows the baits to assume a natural orientation in the water that facilitates a lifelike swimming motion. The baits are also impregnated with natural finishes and holographic flash that replicate many different prey baits. This combination of features work in concert, along with an effective retrieve, to generate a significant level of interest from many sport fish. Anglers have enjoyed success with these baits in all parts of the world. On the home front

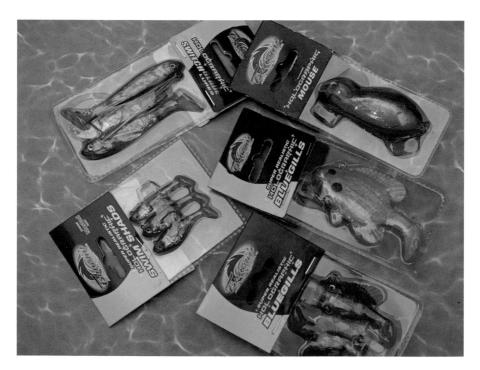

Soft plastic swim baits can be molded in many shapes and sizes.

where I fish in the Northeast, swim baits appear in the tackle bags and surf bags of most anglers who fish for striped bass. At certain times of the year like the fall migration when striped bass run the beaches to feed on shallow masses of baitfish, swim baits are unbeatable for their effectiveness. At times the match between the real bait and the artificial is uncanny for size, shape, coloration, and movement. This connection is most apparent when bass are feeding on peanut bunker, or immature menhaden, in the near surf close to the shoreline. The fish will vigorously strike at the plastic baits, even when fished among the real bunker.

While soft plastic baits have been innovations benefitting from the growth of bass fishing, hard plastic baits have also undergone transformations with the objective of creating smarter artificial lures. Segmentation and articulation have been cornerstones of new-age hard baits. This focus has become a receptive medium for the new paints and finishes that transmit more lifelike imagery. Size of baits has also been on the upswing. The industry is seeing more hard plastic baits being designed for the tough conditions of offshore fishing for large and often select species of fish. For example, anglers are catching tuna regularly on large topwater plugs that embody in their designs the best of lure manufacturing technology. Even tried-and-true tuna jigs that have been the mainstay of that fishery for decades have undergone major facelifts to make them more appealing to tunas through the use of hi-tech materials, laser-sharpened hooks, realistic paint finishes, and hydro-dynamic designs.

All aspects of modern-day smart-lure design rely heavily on contemporary manufacturing techniques that embrace science and cutting-edge technology as part of product development efforts. Whether the focus of attention is on soft plastic baits, hard baits, or other forms of artificial lures, the freshwater bass industry at some point had its influence impact upon new generations of baits by raising the bar on both lure design and effectiveness. Recreational fishing owes much to the world of black bass for creating an environment where continual improvement of baits is now the accepted standard of excellence.

CHAPTER 10

THE PERFECT LURE . . . WELL, ALMOST

The quest to find the mystical Fountain of Youth has obsessed mankind for as long as humans realized their time on this earth was finite. Despite advancements in medicine and science that have extended our lives, the goal of stopping and reversing the aging process has yet to be reached. Yet, many believe the answer lies in the magical waters of a supernatural fountain. While it is the leanest of odds that provide the motivation to continue this eternal search, some intrepid souls refuse to abandon the mission for the miraculous. So it can also be said that for as long as anglers have attempted to catch fish with artificial lures, it has been their quest to discover the elusive and mystical perfect lure. Whether anglers fish with hard baits, soft baits, or flies, their goal remains the same: To discover artificial baits that consistently, if not always, get fish to bite. But as all seasoned anglers know, that lofty objective is rarely a reality. Some lures do indeed come close to perfection under certain conditions and with specific species of fish, but finding a "one size fits all" artificial lure would be like finding the Holy Grail.

As part of my own quest to understand the degree of perfection anglers might expect from an artificial lure, I sought the opinions of numerous folks who are prominent in the world of recreational angling. Some are involved in contemporary lure design, some are involved in the science of engineering new and improved baits, and some are otherwise involved in the business of sport fishing. Collectively, their insights on modern baits not only shed light on specific hi-tech product trends, but also on the sophistication of modern fishing lures. The benefit of their experience in lure design, materials, and the application of scent help increase one's rate of hooking and catching fish.

One of the most talented and inventive lure designers that I had contacted and interviewed several years back for a series of articles I was writing on the subject of modern lure development is Patrick Sebile, founder of Sebile Lures. He is a master angler and master lure designer whose extraordinary list of angling accomplishments is well documented. Over the years, Sebile has seen much more science applied to the design of contemporary fishing lures, and he has embraced that science in the development of his own line of lures. Sebile believes that when designing lures, one needs to look at the implications of both active feeding conditions and those fishing times when feeding activity is at the slowest. Sebile has designed lures to perform under many fishing conditions, but especially so when fish are inactive or not feeding at all. According to Sebile, the real challenge of a lure maker is to motivate passive fish to eat. To be effective at this, a thorough understanding of fish behaviors and habits is the critical key to designing effective lures. Sebile suggests that the way in which fish often hone in on bait is through their lateral lines. When a fish gets close to the bait, its sense of sight kicks in to make certain of the target and to decide how it will attack and grab the prey. He has also offered that "the value of plastic baits is that they present a very natural underwater signature of a real life form."

Conceptually, the key attributes of soft-sided baits lie in their ability to have specific interactions with water that allow for the creation of subtle, life-like "waves" which generate low-level vibrations. These baits are able to make water move around them naturally. Sebile added:

> The Sebile Soft Magic Swimmer was designed to replicate as closely as possible natural bait in the form of size, color, action, and the turbulence it creates in the water. The realistic swimming action of the bait comes as a result of the proper relationship between shape, length, and the result of the lure's opposing forces against the water. To achieve this, lure designers must closely study how fish and bait move, the way they propel themselves, and use propulsion to swim. Another critical element in lure design is that shape and balance must work in concert with one another. The turbulence created by that balance of dimensions influences water pressure and causes the bait to move one way and then the other. The most effective baits "swim" with underwater waves and disturbances that attract fish.

During his guiding days, Sebile ran a series of controlled experiments with his clients. Using similar and dissimilar baits under equal and diverse conditions, he observed the following. Success at catching was color-dependent 30 percent of the time; while 70 percent of catch rate success was keyed to size, action, and shape of the artificial baits. In many instances, specific configurations and use of baits caught specific species. There were also baits that caught the most fish while other artificials caught the biggest fish. Another observation was that on some days action that replicated real prey worked the best, while on other days, dramatic departures from realistic movements attracted the most bites.

Patrick offered a valuable message to all anglers: "Keep an open mind regarding what you tie on to your line and be willing to experiment. Too many anglers simply depend on too few confidence lures, and while they may be excellent anglers, catch rates could be enhanced by experimenting." The hardest thing for a lure manufacturer to understand is what fish actually feel and sense when stimulated by a particular bait. That is the ultimate challenge and the one I most want to understand. A lure designer has to translate what a fish senses into the design of a bait and create an underwater signature that is as close as possible to the real signals.

Soft baits have certainly burst onto both the freshwater and saltwater fishing scene. Jerry Gomber is the Director of Development, Performance Products for Bimini Bay Outfitters, and he has offered some insights on the effectiveness of their Tsunami line of soft baits. Gomber believes that there are a few specifics about why soft baits work so well: "They present a prey species silhouette in a variety of shapes and sizes; some have extraordinarily lifelike action on the fall and on retrieve; the best have both front body and tail swimming actions; they offer a variety of presentation options—jig, cast/retrieve, troll, etc." Gomber adds that novice anglers can be successful on a very short learning curve since these lures can be effective with simple cast and retrieve techniques:

> Whether the soft baits utilize a hook-and-weight configuration or bodies added to a weighted head, anglers can present these baits anywhere in the water column. Some extra-heavy models are designed for either deep presentations or for effective use in currents. Manufacturers can deliver colors and patterns that match forage species or stark contrast patterns to attract predators. Soft

Constant innovation is a characteristic of all top-tier lure designers.

baits also have a "real" feel when mouthed by predators. In a predominantly single-hook bait, this is important. Predators tend to hold the lure that important instant longer. Some use scent or other chemical attractants can also be valuable for creating greater appeal of a soft bait.

William "Doc" Muller holds a PhD in biology with a specialty in marine sciences. In addition to having been a marine sciences professor at the New York Institute of Technology, Muller is an avid angler, prolific writer, and book author. Doc is legendary surf fisherman on his home waters of Long Island, and in particular the waters of the Long Island Sound. Muller routinely applies scientific thinking as part of his fishing strategies and tactics. And Dr. Muller believes the perfect lure may already exist in the form of a bucktail. His primary reasoning is that the bucktail is a "non-niche" artificial lure, meaning that it is not a species-specific lure, nor is it an artificial bait that can only be fished in one level of the water column. The conditions under which a bucktail can be fished are many and varied, and it is a lure that has proven effective for countless species of game fish. Doc Muller attributes the universal success of the bucktail to what he calls a, "symphony of attributes" that allow the bait, with the appropriate angler-generated retrieve action, to effectively imitate dying, sickly, or struggling prey bait. He suggests that when fishing a bucktail, the angler should endeavor to "think" like the fish and its behaviors under varying sets of conditions, in essence asking: "What would a fish do under these circumstances, and how can I better manipulate the bucktail to make it easy for the fish to eat?" It is also imperative that the angler understands how the bucktail behaves when under the influences of varying water conditions.

Furthermore, a bucktail's versatility is its most significant characteristic, making it an almost universal bait, and when taken to the next level, the basic bucktail can indeed transform into a smarter lure. A bucktail is built off a main body structure comprised of a jig head (the weight of which can vary) affixed to a long shank hook (the size of which also varies). In its most original and primitive form, a luremaker ties white bucktail directly onto the hook at the juncture point where the jig head meets the hook shank. Over time, luremakers painted the standard lead jig to give it more of a natural and appealing look. Painted and prismatic eyes likewise give somewhat greater realism. Eventually bucktail builders embraced the sophistication of modern hi-tech materials and synthetics. Tying techniques, often borrowed from the fly-tying community, enhanced the way in which materials were attached to the bucktail hook. This allowed for more creative, lifelike, and effective lures and presentations. One enterprising fabricator of these lures is John Paduano, who produces a line of products known as Premium Bucktails. In essence, Paduano applies the best of contemporary bucktail techniques, fly tying, materials, and methods to his bucktail-making process. Paduano believes that "many excellent fishermen, when given the choice of selecting only one lure for all of their fishing, opt for the bucktail jig. It is perhaps the ultimate fish-catching tool, effective in a wide range of conditions and on virtually every species that swims. There is also a certain amount of satisfaction derived from catching fish on a lure that is dependent on your ability to impart the correct action." Paduano's quest to find the perfect bucktail began when he realized that many of the standard bucktails on the market weren't up to his liking with respect to materials, color, and quality control. His bucktail epiphany occurred many years back while fishing for

Many anglers believe the bucktail to be the most versatile of all artificial baits.

striped bass on a Long Island jetty. The bass were feeding on tinker mackerel, but none of the bucktails at the time were up to the task of stimulating a strike. It struck him at the time that if he could "match the hatch" as fly tyers do, his efforts might be rewarded with more receptive fish. So Paduano crafted a number of bucktails tied to represent mackerel and ventured back to the jetty. Bass that were reluctant to eat the day before aggressively hit the much-improved bucktail. From that point on Paduano began to tie many varieties of bucktails to imitate other bait fish species. His track record is exemplary, accounting for more than 150 species of sport fish all along the east coast and in Central America. Their realism makes this smarter bucktail more effective in clear water. Like contemporary hard and soft baits, John's Premium Bucktails utilize the best of matched saddle hackles, modern 3D eyes, laser-sharpened hooks, high-quality synthetic materials, and durable flex-coat finishes.

Gary Abernathy is the marketing manager for LIVETARGET Lures. When talking with him about the "perfect" lure, Abernathy suggested that LIVETARGET's mantra is a philosophy that guides their lure production to utilize all attributes of modern technology to design and engineer lures that most accurately reflect nature. This operating principle efforts to replicate nature as closely as possible by representing anatomical accuracy and how baitfish actually move in the water. Abernathy adds that this approach then enables a predatory fish to see a realistic image of prey as it homes in on specific artificial baits. In essence, this concept, as it pertains to hard and soft baits, is an extension of the long-held practice when fly fishing for trout to "match the hatch." Trout can be highly selective, and their discriminating palate applies to all life-cycle-stages of their favorite aquatic insects and flies. Whether that stage be as larvae, nymph, or fully-emerged fly, trout will more often than not focus on a specific type of food, of a specific size, and feed in a frustratingly choosy manner. When this happens, only anglers who are able to match those feeding preferences and select a fly that embodies all the attributes of the natural food will find success. Abernathy suggests that LIVETARGET Lures achieve the same end result of matching the prevalent baitfish by offering a variety of artificial baits that are visually accurate, display a true underwater signature of the bait's action, and are weight-balanced for ideal casting and retrieving mechanics. This last consideration is crucial for Abernathy, since he further suggests that it is the thinking angler who understands the forage bait and actively works to mimic that bait in the form of an artificial lure to stimulate a fish to strike.

Nick Cicero, sales manager at Tsunami suggests that one of the keys to creating more effective artificial lures is to utilize modern technology to achieve greater durability of baits, especially in the harsher environments of saltwater. Cicero also points out that while it is relatively easy to make a soft bait swim naturally, it is more difficult to make that bait functionally durable. To that end, he cites that modern soft bait designs are now incorporating the use of Kevlar cloth gauze as a means to add greater strength to the lure and

Anatomical realism is a foundation principal for lure designers and manufacturers like LIVETARGET Lures.

extend useful life of that bait by enhancing durability. Cicero also sees a movement toward creating artificial baits that appeal to the ways specific fish species feed. For example, one species might feed primarily through the use of sound and sight senses, while another species will feed by engaging the senses of sight, sound and scent. And then there are those fish that have a highly-developed sense of smell and will utilize that awareness as a primary feeding mechanism. From a purely mechanical engineering perspective Cicero envisions more sophistication in the designs of weight transfer systems. Newer technology will result in greater flight trajectory stability during the cast and truer tracking on the retrieve. These features would be further augmented by more aerodynamic designs that will allow for longer casts.

As anglers look to the future of smart artificial lures, some of the emerging themes for further refining those baits toward perfection appear to be widespread among lure manufacturers. Most indicate that they will place greater emphasis on designs that appeal to most, if not all, the senses that fish use to feed. What that translates to is lures that combine multiple features that not only induce fish to strike a bait when feeding, but to also cause fish to hit a bait that generates other stimuli. Most prominent of these attributes will be those that stimulate the senses of sound, scent, and sight. Some suggest that the combination of those elements will be so significant that new-age artificial lures will be able to attract fish to corridors of travel that will lead them straight to the lure. Some suggest that rather than seek out the fish, the fish will find the angler. A number of key developments are taking place to refine the way in which science adds to the overall effectiveness of smart artificial baits. Those advancements include: soft baits constructed of bio-degradable materials; designs that blend the best attributes of both hard and soft baits; enhanced utilization of scent to more accurately replicate pheromones that cause fish to feed and strike a bait; and bio-mechanical technologies and devices like micro chips that work to emit electrical impulses, sound, and light to trigger reaction strikes. Innovation of bait texture will also become a more prevalent design aspect. This is especially relevant with soft baits, where plastics can easily be molded to accurate representations of the sizes and shapes of various baits. Taking that attribute a step further, soft bait designs will evolve to a point where the texture of soft baits will be engineered to match the consistency and feel of the natural baits. An artificial bait's texture will also affect the action of that bait and how it swims and behaves when retrieved.

In reality, the quest to achieve a more perfect lure is limited only by the imagination of those who design artificial baits, and by the creative application of modern technology. The infusion of science into modern production is no doubt here to stay and should only become more prevalent as the years advance. To that end, baits will continue to become smarter, more productive, and more efficient. Mike Laptew is a renowned New England angler and underwater videographer who has spent much time viewing and filming fish in their element. When we spoke about the goal to achieve perfection in an artificial lure, Laptew summed up the interrelationship of critical design factors in this way: "Size, shape, and action are of primary importance, while sound, color, and scent play supporting roles. The most effective lures create a symphony of those elements." One can only speculate about the future of smart baits and how science and technology will further impact the sport. It is not beyond the realm of possibility that artificial intelligence could eventually be embedded into artificial lures via micro chips or small computing devices to make them behave in ways that simulate the natural responses of bait fish and other prey. Regardless of when or how this might happen, one certainty is that lure designers and manufacturers will always strive for continual improvement in the quest to achieve realism and perfection of smart baits. But if smart anglers do not find desired attributes in their factory manufacturers' lures, they will modify and adapt those baits as needed.

I have known Bob Daly for many years. We first met two and half decades ago at a remote fishing lodge on the Alaska Peninsula where the silver salmon fishing is as good as it gets. Throughout the years, Bob and I would annually meet up in the wilds of the Alaska Peninsula to chase large, feisty cohos, char, Dolly Varden, and rainbow trout. As I got to know Bob and we became friends, it became apparent to me that he is a fisherman's fisherman, expanding his involvement in the sport well beyond the scope of Alaska. Bob has fished throughout the world at some of the most exotic and remote fishing holes on this planet, places most anglers only visit in their dreams, such as Tanzania, Uganda, Suriname, Venezuela, Brazil, China, Argentina, the Maldives, and Papua New Guinea for exotic species of large, tackle-busting fish. Some of the out-of-the-ordinary species he has to his credit include gargantuan Redtail Catfish, Barramundi, Featherbacks, Tigerfish, Nile Perch, Papua New Guinea Bass, Golden Dorado, and Lau Lau. Bob is primarily a lure fisherman, and he employs some exceptionally large plugs for the monster fish that he targets. In consideration of all the species that

Large modern plugs have been the key to success for Bob Daly's exotic game fish exploits. CREDITS: BOB DALY.

Bob has under his belt, I asked him about his views on lure design and what characteristics he considers most important in a lure. Without hesitation Bob replied, "action and vibration." When you take into account that many of the waters that Bob has fished in foreign lands have been muddied and off color, appealing to a fish's senses of sound has been the key to strikes. Bob also revealed that he rarely, if ever, fishes a lure directly out of the box without first tweaking it. He indicated to me that he will spend days of lure preparation, doctoring and customizing each lure to meet his standards for whatever species he is targeting, and to ensure that it swims in a manner that will attract attention. One interesting example for large peacock bass, is that he labors the propeller spin to get it just right on the plugs he uses. Over the course of many trips to the Brazilian Amazon, Bob has found that just the right pitch and angle of a propeller generates a sputter and splash that appeals most to the peacock bass. Since the stock lure does not have that exact propeller orientation, he adjusts each lure to his unique specifications before using it.

Larry Dahlberg is a legendary figure in the recreational sport fishing industry. He is a recognized expert in all forms of angling and styles of equipment. His "Hunt for Big Fish" television show captivated and educated anglers for more than two decades, and his passion for lure design and lure manufacturing has led to the creation of some truly unique and very effective artificial lures and flies. Dalhberg is also known as a lifelong inventor and tackle and lure tinkerer. Within the fly fishing community, his Dahlberg Diver has proven to be one of the most innovative, effective, and original creations to have ever come off a fly-tying vise, and within the realm of more conventional artificial baits, his Whopper Plopper enjoys tremendous success with many large species of game fish I was very delighted when Larry agreed to talk with me about this book and his lure design concepts.

Right out of the box, the first thing Dahlberg said to me was that anglers need to recognize that there are two fundamental types of fish: those that eat bugs and such, and those that eat other fish and other forms of aquatic life. In the context of that belief, Dahlberg further suggested that some fish are physiologically hard-wired to eat insects, while that other segment is similarly hard-wired to eat each other. Those predispositions will guide an angler's selection of an artificial lure and the methods and techniques used to impart appropriate action to those baits. Larry further suggested that there are two things to consider when designing or selecting an artificial bait: What does the lure look like, and, what does the lure do? For example, presenting a fly offering to a bug eater under the "what does it look like scenario" takes into consideration variables different from feeding a plug or other style lure to a fish-eater. Dahlberg offers that he has "dead drifted an object [fly or replica of food] in a non-threatening way into the cubic holding and feeding space of a fish and has had that object eaten most times. Yet, in contrast, if we move to the opposite end of the spectrum to where the predatory fish eaters dwell, the strike-triggering qualities of an artificial bait take on different traits." Dahlbergh postulates that in this instance how a lure reacts in the presence of predators is the critical factor. The goal is to make the lure look lifelike to the fish. There is a big difference between what a fish sees and what an angler sees. The physical properties of water and air differ vastly and affect how an image is perceived. So the objective is to approximate as much as is reasonably possible the view and the experience from the fish's point of view. As a master lure maker, Dahlberg offers this: "I make lures based on what that lure can do, not based on what it looks like." Dahlberg also referenced the concept of random mechanical action in lures and the importance that characteristic plays in stimulating fish to strike. Fundamentally, what constitutes this capability can best be described by Dahlberg as a little "hitch" in the retrieve, aided by incremental action that is imparted by the angler. Simply put, the combination of a built-in hitch to the lure's action plus an angler's ability to retrieve the lure in a stimulating fashion, increases the odds of fish striking that bait. Envision a topwater lure moving along at a singular and steady pace, with monotone sounds being emitted

Larry Dahlberg's passion for lure design has led to the development of many innovative and effective artificial baits, including his novel "Whopper Plopper." CREDIT: LARRY DAHLBERG

from that bait. Now take that same bait, tweak it to where it has a slight hitch or twitch to its action, modify the retrieve to vary how it pushes water, and you have an entirely new presentation, one that appeals much more to a fish's strike instincts.

Dahlberg also suggests that fish are food samplers that will take in and reject items that are not suitable sources of food, and ultimately eat that which is consistent with their diet. And in the process of sampling, the more appealing a lure can be to tempt the curiosity of the fish, the more bites it will generate. Furthermore, the more a lure also appeals to the process of natural selection, the more effective it can be. One classic example of this is when fish are seemingly feeding selectively on one specific type of bait. Anglers anguish over precisely matching the lure to the bait. But often it is the counter approach of presenting a lure that stands out from the pack and is dissimilar to the natural that gets the attention of fish. While there are many presumed rationales for this behavior, it is reasonable to suggest that standing out from the pack suggests vulnerability in the context of natural selection, and that triggers a predatory reaction strike.

The methods of fishing artificial lures typically involve a decision-making progression. One of the related topics that Dahlberg and I discussed was his overall view of the fishing process and how he navigates the route toward the selection of a specific bait or set of baits. Dahlberg views this process in the context of three related and integrated elements: Mechanics; Strategy; and Tactics. Within the framework of these three component parts, "mechanics" relate to that with the angler can control. This would include things like the tackle choices—spinning, fly or conventional. Strategy would relate to an overarching plan of action that is most appropriate for the options that are presented by the environment. For example, moving water, still water, heavy structure, beach, sloughs, flats, types of bait, targeted species, etc. And lastly, tactics drill down to the specifics of the angler's approach and choice of lures to achieve the end-game of getting a fish to eat. Applying this methodology to one's fishing will only work to enhance the overall experience and result in more successful outings.

CHAPTER 11

ART OF THE RETRIEVE

As we have seen, contemporary anglers have at their disposal some of the best artificial lures ever designed. In many cases, those lures are as anatomically identical as possible to the baitfish they are designed to imitate. But no matter how realistic a hard or soft bait may be, it can't, for all practical purposes, catch fish on its own. Any artificial bait must be brought to life by angler intervention before it can be expected to stimulate a fish to strike. This involvement comes about through the process of a retrieve. The goal of any fishing retrieve is to create deception and to persuade a game fish that a fraudulent bait is real and something both vulnerable and edible.

When I was writing my first fly pattern book, *Saltwater Flies of the Northeast,* a well-known New England fly tier sent me samples of his flies along with a fishing tip to include in the book. His note was simple, profound, and on the mark, and applies not only to flies but to all forms of artificial baits as well: "I'd rather fish the wrong fly right, than fish the right fly wrong." The same principle applies to hard and soft baits. The way in which an angler "works" a lure can spell the difference between success and failure. What often goes unnoticed among some anglers, especially those new to the game, is that there is no "Holy Grail" lure. How an angler fishes and manipulates a bait, regardless of how spectacular or "smart" that bait may appear, can most often mean the difference between hooking fish and just engaging in some casting practice. That is where the effectiveness of a retrieve is critical.

The purpose of the retrieve is to make the artificial bait appear as a natural imitation of a real life form. The angler must cause the lure to behave as if it is alive, injured, or vulnerable. Changing up the retrieve to provide different "looks" at a bait is a way to accomplish that. Just as a baseball pitcher changes up on the speed or action of a baseball to confuse a batter, the same effect can be achieved with fish by changing up the retrieve of a lure. The way in which an artificial bait appears to a fish can also be affected by the choice of lines, leader materials, knots, and any form of swivel or clip. In many instances it is the subtlest of details that determine how well a lure will fish. Some anglers go to great lengths to customize and fine tune lures to achieve a desired action when retrieved. Yet even the best lures don't always produce as expected. And when that happens, the first inclination of many anglers is to change lures or try a different color, or both. But there is one tactical principle that anglers should employ before snipping that lure off the line: Change the retrieve before changing lures. Regardless of a lure's appeal or Imposter Quotient, the way in which an angler fishes that lure will be the determining factor in its success. Yet there are a number of variables that affect the effectiveness of a retrieve.

LINES

Line diameter is an important element to consider when imparting the desired action to a hard or soft bait, and with flies and teasers. The larger the diameter of a line and leader the more resistance it has when descending the water column and the more it can potentially impede the movement of lures, especially light lures, when tied direct without the use of a swivel or clip. Small-diameter lines also offer a casting advantage by allowing a lure to be propelled to greater distances. Older-generation monofilament lines and some contemporary lines have a linear correlation between line diameters and pound-test ratings: the larger the diameter, the higher the strength rating of the line. Braid lines offer a unique advantage in that their diameters relative to monofilament are smaller for equal pound-test ratings. So the diameter of a thirty-pound test braid is approximately equivalent to that of eight-pound test monofilament. The benefits of that relationship are obvious: the casting and lure manipulation attributes of light line, and the strength of heavier pound-test. Modern technology has also allowed the extruding process for manufacturing monofilament to produce thinner, softer, and more supple lines that work to enhance lure action. Fluorocarbon lines and hybrid monofilament lines also offer other fishing advantages. Fluorocarbon provides a degree of "invisibility" when immersed in water, so there is less of a tendency for wary species of fish to become line shy and spook. Fluorocarbon also offers more abrasion resistance, and that allows fishing in areas where dense cover or structure pose a risk. Knots are also an important consideration with respect to the action of a lure. Absent swivels or clips, a knot that allows a lure or fly to swing will enhance the action of that bait. One of the best knots for this application is the non-slip knot, which creates a loop that lets the lure move freely and unimpeded. Other knots can tend to hinder a lure's action when cinched up against the hook eye. Also bear in mind that some knots are better than others for use with the different types of line: monofilament, fluorocarbon, hybrid, and braid. For example, the texture and composition of braided lines has lead to the development of "braid specific" knots like the Berkley Braid Knot, which create more secure connection between the line and lures, and the braid and leaders.

Within the realm of fly fishing, line types and weights are critical components for effective casting and retrieving. With more traditional fishing methods like spinning or bait casting, it is the weight of the lure that pulls lines from the reel. With fly fishing, the line acts as the propellant to move the fly during the cast. But line variations can also help the angler manage the way in which a fly is presented to fish. Floating lines will keep a fly in the upper levers of the water column; intermediate lines will move a fly to the mid-levels; and high density sinking lines will allow the fly to approach the lower portions of water near the bottom. Choice of lines will also impact upon certain retrieve techniques such as mending line and swinging flies in current; methods used to keep a fly moving in a natural manner. Fly material and fly construction will also affect how a fly performs. Materials such as marabou, rabbit, and long, supple hackles will generate a more seductive flowing effect during a retrieve or drift.

As with hard and soft baits, no fly is magic. Granted, there may be days when a particular pattern or lure will outshine all others and give the impression that it is the answer to all your fishing dreams, but that could all change with the next cast. The key to unlocking the illusionary charm of any artificial bait is an intelligent approach to retrieves.

SMART RETRIEVES

Many anglers very often rely on one favorite retrieve for all fishing situations. Inexperienced anglers especially will simply cast out a lure and then retrieve it back in as if performing a rote procedure. When it comes to retrieves, "one size does not fit all." Keeping a lure moving at only one rate of speed, and without any variation to its motion may work at times, but it is often like listening to a monotone monologue: tedious and boring. Variety may be the spice of life but when retrieving an artificial bait, variation brings a lure to life. Additionally, varied retrieves are often better at effectively working some baits than others. Also, some fish respond differently to specific retrieves. Consistently successful anglers learn to give fish different "looks" under different conditions and circumstances, and to adapt their retrieves to the prevalent fishing scenarios. The following retrieves are ones every angler should keep in his or her bag of tricks. These retrieves can be adapted to conventional casting methods or to fly fishing.

Slow and Steady

The simplest of all retrieves is to get the lure or fly in motion with a slow gathering of line. This method is often most productive when trying to give the impression of a slowly-meandering bait or one that is in the final stages of life. Interspersed pauses also make this retrieve effective. It works well with casting and spinning gear and with swimming plugs fished on the surface or when crawling a bait along the bottom. When used in fly fishing, this technique involves grasping the fly line and steadily drawing line back in long, slow pulls of eighteen to twenty-four inches. The retrieve is further enhanced by pausing between pulls. That temporary halt allows the fly to move a distance, stop and then move again. The long slow pull retrieve can also be alternated with more rapid pulls and pauses. When the rate of retrieve is varied in that fashion it adds more a lifelike motion to the fly. Fish will hit on the pull, the pause, or at the point when the fly is put in motion.

Fast and Erratic

This is an alternative retrieve to the slow-and-steady technique. When employed, a fast-and-erratic movement gives the impression of a fleeing baitfish, and that can trigger a reaction strike from fish. Although we cannot know what response mechanisms ignite within the brain of a fish, we do know that a fast-and-erratic retrieve with occasional pauses does indeed stimulate a fish's senses to pursue the bait and strike. In saltwater, a retrieve of this nature works well for fast-swimming fish like tuna, little tunny, bonito, most mackerel, and bluefish.

Short and Slow

Short gathering of line with traditional casting and spinning gear or short pulls of line with fly tackle influence this retrieve. Alternating between a slow movement of the bait and periodic pauses adds extra appeal. Fish will often hit on the pause or as the lure begins to move once the retrieve is resumed. Combinations of varying retrieve speeds will add even more allure to the bait's motion.

Wrist Flick

This motion can be employed with any of the previous retrieves and with any form of tackle. It involves imparting a periodic wrist-flicking motion during the retrieve. This action causes the lure to dart about as if it is baitfish that has been injured or that is trying to escape. Very often game fish will strike the lure or fly in response to the darting motion, the pause, or the transition back to a swimming motion. I was first shown this technique many years ago while fly fishing for blackwater tarpon, but it works equally as well for other fish species that respond well to this motion.

Combination Retrieves

Fish will respond differently to specific retrieves. It often takes some experimentation to determine the retrieve that will stimulate fish to strike a fly. Preferences can vary from day to day. One of the best ways to test the reaction of fish is by mixing up retrieves and combining techniques. For example, if a simple, long pull retrieve isn't working, try a long-and-short pull in combination with a fast-and-slow retrieve or a wrist flick.

FLY-SPECIFIC SMART RETRIEVE TECHNIQUES
Figure Eight Crawl

This non-traditional technique is one that I've borrowed from freshwater trout fishing when retrieving dry flies or nymphs that have been cast upstream and allowed to flow naturally with the current. The retrieve works well in saltwater when fishing with crab or crustacean patterns on or near the bottom, and when trying to imitate a natural crawling action. It is ideal for fish feeding on thin-water sand or mud flats, or shallow areas with rocks and gravel. With this retrieve method the angler makes a cast and then places line between the thumb and forefinger. Rotating the wrist and gathering line with the lower three fingers moves the fly along in small increments.

Double Overhand Retrieve

This retrieve is ideal for moving a fly rapidly through the water. It is very effective for fast-moving pelagic species of fish like Atlantic bonito, little tunny, and Spanish mackerel. Other game fish will also respond to the retrieve when feeding on fast-moving bait. With this technique the angler places the rod under the armpit and uses two hands to retrieve the fly, gathering with a motion that moves the hands one over the other to move the fly through the water. This method requires a different hook set that has the angler strip set by simultaneously pulling on the line and vigorously lifting the rod.

Mending Line

One line management technique that is of value to the surf fly angler is mending. This method works best in moving water where the fly is fished in a naturally-drifting fashion, floating unimpeded with the movement of current. While mending was first used when fly-fishing for steelhead, salmon, and trout in rivers, it holds an important place in the surf angler's retrieve arsenal. What this technique entails is casting the fly up-current and as it flows through the course of the drift, picking line up off the water and moving that line back upstream. This accomplishes three things: it allows the fly to drift naturally with the current—the fly is not at all restrained by line tension—and the fly can remain in the strike zone longer. Fish may see this as a bait form just moving with the flow of water. The inherent action of the fly drifting in this manner will motivate fish to strike, as will the terminal point of the drift where the line eventually tightens and the fly moves up the water column. Mending line is an integral part of the "greased line" fishing technique, where the goal is to present the broad profile or silhouette to fish. The method works quite well when fishing rips, areas of tidal current, and the tips of jetties.

Line Contact

Whether engaged in the act of casting or retrieving, it is essential for an angler to always maintain constant contact with the line. This is vital regardless of the form of tackle used. Only by staying in touch with the line can an angler maintain a connection with the lure and know how that lure is behaving during the retrieve. Losing contact with a lure will, more often than not, result in missed hook sets and missed fish. Contact with line extends from the cast, to the retrieve, and through to the hook set. This three-part link is especially significant when fishing and manipulating artificial baits. Braided lines changed up the game dramatically with respect to feeling what a lure or bait is doing and for detecting even the subtlest strikes. While monofilament and fluorocarbon lines offer their own unique characteristics and opportunities, braided line can offer a high degree of sensitivity and "feel." The more an angler can sense how a lure behaves during the retrieve, the more that will add to the overall performance of hard and soft smart baits. Fishermen who bottom-bounce lures like bucktails, jigs and soft plastics want minimal stretch and maximum sensitivity, and many find that braided lines deliver on both those attributes, as well as generating more hook sets. This offers an especially meaningful advantage when fishing in deeper water. Lines with less stretch are able to better transmit the most delicate bites. Working lures on the surface or at other levels of the water column is also more efficient when maintaining an active connection between angler, line, and lure.

CHAPTER 12

WHAT'S YOUR LINE

The most critical connection in fishing is that which exists between the lure and the angler. That link is made possible by the line. No matter how smart or effective a bait may be, unless that bait is influenced in a positive way by a proper retrieve it will never be as productive as it could be. While an angler's ability to manipulate an artificial bait is paramount, the choice of line one uses is of equal, if not greater significance.

During the winter of 2017, I moderated a panel of prominent anglers, writers, and science professionals as part of a Long Island, NY fishing exposition, all of whom fish and are involved in the recreational sport fishing industry. One person asked the entire panel to choose what they thought was the most significant contribution to recreational sport fishing over the past two decades. The almost unanimous response was the innovations made to fishing lines, specifically braided line. In the past few decades, manufacturers have made dramatic improvements to all forms of fishing lines. The recreational fishing industry has come a very long way from the catgut lines used in the 1600s and silk lines that became popular in the 1700s. With the advent of bait-casting gear in the Unites States came linen and braided silk lines, and eventually braided Dacron lines dominated the scene, especially within the realm of bait casting.

Spinning reels ushered in the age of monofilament, constructed from a single strand of nylon. Since the introduction of "mono," that line type has undergone a beneficial evolution well rooted in changing technology. There are supple monofilament lines that help to improve casting distance, abrasion-resistant lines that can be fished in heavy cover and inhospitable structure, and low-visibility lines that mask the presence of the line in clear water. Manufacturers build fluorocarbon lines from a single strand of polyvinylidene fluoride. This line type has gained considerably in popularity among anglers for its low-visibility qualities in clear water. Fluorocarbon

Modern lines have come a long way since the days of first-generation braid, dacron lines, and silk gut leaders.

also requires more applied force for it to stretch than does monofilament, an attribute that assists greatly in the process of hook-setting as well as increased sensitivity. This line also has a high level of abrasion resistance, provides solid knot-tying capabilities, and is resistant to the effects of UV light. Fluorocarbon has also become a favored material for building leaders, especially for the harsh conditions dished out in saltwater environments. The fly-fishing community has also embraced fluorocarbon, particularly for leaders used in shallow, clear water for fish species that are line shy and spook easily. The low stretch feature of fluoro aids with the strip-strike method used in saltwater.

Early monofila-
ment lines played
a major role in the
popularity of
spinning and
spin-casting
tackle.

Along with the advancement of monofilament and fluorocarbon, and the relevant features/benefits of both line types, has also come the development of hybrid line that marries the best attributes of both line types. Hybrid lines are referred to as co-polymer lines that are basically a blend of different materials. This cross between mono and fluoro offers the best of both worlds for certain fishing applications. For example, some anglers prefer this form of hybrid line when spin-fishing for inshore saltwater pelagic species like little tunny, Atlantic bonito, Spanish mackerel, and small bluefin tuna. In these situations hybrid lines offer the suppleness of monofilament, which aids casting distance, and fluorocarbon's invisibility factor and toughness. The lines also have applications in any number of freshwater fishing situations where suppleness and toughness are desired characteristics.

Beyond the monofilament and the fluorocarbon is a microfilament-based line that has been so revolutionary it has changed the industry. This line is referred to as braided line. Although anglers used cotton, linen, and silk casting lines during the early days of recreational fishing, new-age braided lines utilize hi-tech materials to create products that are a far cry from the braids of old. It is the nature of the contemporary materials used that contributes to the popularity of braid in both freshwater and saltwater fishing. Modern braids weave strong fiber materials like Spectra, Dacron, or Dyneema. These polymers have characteristics that make them highly desirable as components of fishing lines. Braided lines made from those products have a number of beneficial characteristics, including much smaller diameters for similar breaking strength than their monofilament or fluorocarbon counterparts, often as much as third to quarter of the diameter. This translates to more braided line on a spool than monofilament or fluorocarbon. This feature is especially significant when fishing for big-game species or fish that make long runs after being hooked. The small diameter-to-breaking-strength ratio of braid also allows for the use of more compact reels, since a smaller reel spool can hold sufficient line. For this reason, braided lines are also often used as backing on fly reels in lieu of more traditional Dacron. Once again, this is particularly relevant when fishing for game fish that make long, sustained runs. Small-diameter braid also facilitates longer distance casting by unspooling more easily and by offering less air resistance, all without sacrificing line strength. The polymers used in the manufacture of braid create a very abrasion-resistant line. This is advantageous to anglers who fish in heavy cover and around abrasive structure such as rocks, boulders, docks, and sunken wreck.

Modern braid lines have been instrumental in advancing the design of both fishing tackle and artificial lures.

Another of the beneficial features of braid is its virtual lack of any significant stretch. This has the advantage of allowing for a more forceful and direct hook set. Anglers like freshwater bass fishermen and saltwater bottom fishermen especially appreciate this attribute. This quality also enables an angler to stay in constant contact with not only the line but with the terminal rig as well. Where sensitivity and feel matters, braided lines offer a significant advantage. In situations where an element of finesse is required of one's fishing, when feeling subtleties of a strike or sensing what a bait is doing, braided lines can indeed help with more consistent hook sets. But along with all the good that comes with braid, the line type does have a few shortcomings that can be easily overcome. First and foremost, braided line is much more visible in the water than either fluorocarbon or low-visibility monofilament. Therefore fish, especially wary species, may shy away. So the fundamental rigging technique when fishing with braid is to attach a fluorocarbon leader. The length and size of the leader will depend upon the species one is targeting. When fishing for aggressive species like bluefish that will attack just about anything they can get into their mouths, or bottom species where the scent of bait is the overpowering motivator to strike, a short leader will suffice. Longer leaders come into play if one is fishing for smallmouth bass in crystal-clear water, or for trout. Regardless of the species, I like to use enough fluorocarbon that is not only the length of the rod but also wraps several times around the reel spool. Here's a prime example of why a leader is needed when fishing with braid. I was fishing for carp with a friend on a small pond for a total of three mornings. Other than our choices of line, we fished the same baits on identical terminal tackle. My reels were spooled with a hybrid fluorocarbon and monofilament blend, while my friend chose to use braid that he tied directly to his terminal gear. Over the course of those fishing outings I was fortunate to catch five carp between fifteen and twenty pounds and a by-catch of fifteen trout. My friend unfortunately caught zero carp. But the next time we met to fish this pond he had attached a length of fluorocarbon leader to his braided line and proceeded to catch the largest carp of his angling career. Should one take that as experimental proof of a theory? Absolutely not, yet anecdotally and taken at face value, you can't argue with success. This scenario has played out in similar fashion many times since those events unfolded at that small pond.

Braided lines are also relatively slick in texture compared to other lines, and as such they can be more difficult to knot effectively. A result of that slickness is that poorly-tied knots or knots that aren't suitable for braid can slip and possibly become undone. While there are a number of good knots to use with braid, a few of the more popular ones are the Berkley Knot, the Albight Knot, and the Palomar Knot. When tying knots with braided line it is beneficial to add a dab of super glue to the connection. That provides an extra measure of insurance to minimize or prevent any knot slippage. Another consideration when using braided lines is their small diameter, which allows a lot more line to fit on a reel spool than with other forms of line. Sometimes it can be much more line than is practically needed for a particular fishing situation. In those instances, anglers will first pre-load a reel spool with a specific amount of monofilament and then splice in the desired braid, winding it to the desired level on the spool. By doing so, a solid base of line is established and then the appropriate amount of braided line can be added to the spool. This allows for the benefits of braid to be realized, yet limits the waste of any unnecessary line capacity. A further issue when using braid is that this line style can sometimes demonstrate a propensity to tangle when not properly wound back onto the reel with proper line tension. Much of this problem can be avoided by initially winding the braid tightly onto the spool, and continuing to do so after each cast. If the winds are loose, braid has a tendency to dig into the soft accumulation of line mass on the

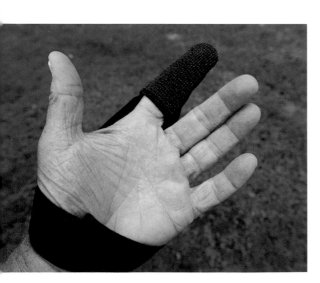

Care must be exercised when using braided line, since their strength and small diameters can easily cut through exposed flesh. Many anglers use protective finger guards.

spool and tangling. Here's one final caveat when using braided line. Due to the line's texture, finish, and diameter, it can more easily cut through materials, including fingers. This is especially relevant if you use an index finger to guide line back onto the reel spool, or when large species of fish make long fast runs, and a finger jut gets in the way. To address this, many anglers will use either some form of tape or a finger glove as protection.

Now that we have examined all the primary line types used for fishing, let's take a quick summary look at comparable features, benefits, and drawbacks. Remember that the correct choice of one's line will only work to improve the overall performance of all hard and soft smart baits.

MONOFILAMENT

Features/Benefits: Monofilament has been around a long time and has become a staple within the recreational fishing community. There are many varieties of "mono" to choose from that meet the demands of varied fishing conditions. Monofilament knots well and maintains effective strength integrity with many knot choices. Mono also comes in varying diameters with different levels of visibility, suppleness, and stretch. It is a good casting line and maintains a reasonable level of abrasion resistance.

FLUOROCARBON

Features/Benefits: Fluorocarbon offers excellent abrasion resistance along with low stretch. Although it is stiffer than monofilament, fluorocarbon line yields low visibility in the water and offers outstanding knot strength. This line is very durable and performs well in dense cover. In addition to its role as a primary line, fluorocarbon has also gained in popularity as a desired leader material, from big-game offshore fishing to finesse fishing for trout.

HYBRID

Features/Benefits: Hybrid lines combine the best features of both monofilament and fluorocarbon, allowing for an alternative line choice that works well under diverse and varied fishing situations.

BRAID

Features/Benefits: Microfilament fibers that produce line diameters less than monofilament fluorocarbon with equal pound-test ratings. Braid also offers the benefit of low stretch and high sensitivity, making subtle strikes more easily detected with more power to the hook set. The limber and pliant nature of braid makes it a great choice for distance casting. Knot slippage and tangles when using braid can be a challenge but solutions to those obstacles are readily available.

FLY LINES

Traditional spinning and casting lines are not the only lines to benefit from technology advancements. Fly lines too have benefitted dramatically from high-tech innovations.

A fly line is one of the most critical pieces of the fly-fishing outfit because it propels the fly to its target. Unlike with spinning or casting tackle that use the weight of a lure or bait to launch the cast, fly fishing relies on the weight of the fly line to thrust the fly toward its goal. Fly lines come in many densities and sizes to match the various conditions and situations that anglers will encounter. Fundamentally, manufacturers create fly line with a durable and strong inner core of monofilament or braid encased in an outer core of resilient plastic. With floating lines, microspheres embedded into the lines add buoyancy. Higher-density substances like lead core are used for full-sinking or sink-tip lines, as well as for shooting heads. The different densities allow for varying sink rates of the line. The heavier grain weight of the sinking portion of a line, the faster that line or tip will sink. For example, a 450-grain tip will sink faster than a 200-grain tip. Likewise, a lighter Type I sink tip will descend slower in the water column than a Type IV. Modern fly line design and construction also incorporates the use of hi-tech coatings on the outer core of the line to create and enhance the slickness of a line, facilitating longer casts.

The primary forms of lines used in fly fishing are: Floating, full sinking, intermediate, and high-density sink tips. Shooting heads are useful for specialty applications. Fly lines also come in different lengths and tapers. Lines of approximately ninety to one hundred feet in length tend to be standard, and weight-forward or double tapers are the two most common tapers. Weight classifications for all practical purposes are assigned to lines and range from 1-weight to 15-weight. Weight in the context of fly lines refers to a measurement in grains. For example, the average grain weight of the head portion of a 1-weight line is 60 grains, while the average mass of a 15-weight head section is 550 grains. Targeted species and fishing conditions govern the weight and type of line an angler uses. For delicate, small-stream trout fishing, an angler might choose a 1–3 weight floating line, while the choice for inshore saltwater fly fishing might call for an 8–11 weight line. Furthermore, a tarpon angler would mostly likely reach for a 12-weight floating line for most fishing conditions and an offshore angler would keep 13–15 weight intermediate tip lines at the ready. Contemporary fly fishing lines are very versatile tools when used to properly fish modern fly patterns.

Floating lines are fully buoyant and are best used when fly presentation is critical, as with dry fly fishing for trout or when fishing top water flies and poppers. Floating lines are also preferable when fishing shallow saltwater areas where longer lines and finer presentations are required, as with tailing bonefish, redfish, or striped bass. Sink tips come in an assortment of densities or weights that descend in the water column at slow, intermediate, and fast sink rates. The line weights are classified in terms of grains, and sink rate in inches per second. Total tip weight is a function of the weight of the core material and the overall length of the tip. Tips can range in length from five to thirty feet. Each rate of descent has application to different surf fishing conditions. I've grown partial to three tip-types that have become the heart of my fishing line arsenal. The first is a high-density fifteen-foot sink tip with a descent rate of about 2.5 to 3.5 inches per second. In stronger currents I will often use a similar length of tip but with a greater sink rate of 3.75 to 4.5 inches per second. A second sink tip is the intermediate clear tip, a favorite of mine for a number of reasons. The slow sink rate makes this tip ideal for fishing along the shoreline edge, or in quieter back-bay areas and flats. This tip style is an alternative to floating lines for fish in skinny water; the slow sink rate and the clear tip is a very effective combination. The clear intermediate tip works especially well in saltwater when fish are mudding for crustaceans, or for fish cruising the flats in search of a meal. One of the benefits of a clear tip is that the tip section can also perform double-duty as a butt extension of the leader. Since the leader tip is clear, you can use a shorter tapered leader or just a straight length of leader tippet. I've often just used four to six feet of straight leader—even with fish like small tuna that have great eyesight—with no ill effects.

The last class of important line tip section are long-length, very high-density tips that sink deep into the water column. Some of the very first of these lines to hit the line market were Jim Teeny's creations. The lines became known simply by their originator's name: Teeny Lines. Other manufacturers have similar lines in their product offerings like Cortland's Quick Descent series. Many of those lines were originally for steelhead and salmon fishing, but were embraced by the saltwater fly fishing community for fishing deep in the water column. My first exposure to Teeny sink tips was in Alaska for Pacific salmon. It was often said back then that if you wanted to catch Alaskan salmon consistently with a fly rod, you needed to learn to cast a Teeny line. These very heavy lines require a change in casting style due to their weight and the fact that you can't efficiently keep all of the line in the air for very long during the casting stroke. The stroke becomes more of a lob than a tight-loop cast. But learning the technique pays handsome dividends for the saltwater fly angler. These high-grain lines can help get a fly into the strike zone when fish are either lying close to the bottom or suspended in deep water. While the previous tip configurations are integrated into the running line, shooting heads are yet another alternative for easily adapting to varying fishing conditions. An angler can switch the "heads" as needed and attached via loop-to-loop connections. A set of shooting heads, each of different weight, is a practical way to achieve effective depth management.

Managing one's presentation of an artificial bait to targeted fish is indeed achieved effectively and efficiently through the use of a proper line. Whether that line is monofilament, braid, hybrid, or fly, making the correct choice is critical to maximizing the bait's productivity. Many substantial improvements to fishing line have taken place over the last few decades. With improvements garnered from advances in science and manufacturing processes, line should continue to improve alongside the continual innovation of smart baits.

CHAPTER 13

RODS, REELS, AND SMART BAITS

There was a time not too long ago when the rod and reel was an angler's primary purchase. The decision-making process usually involved first determining the type of fishing you'd primarily be doing, and then the specific species of fish that you would target. After all, you wouldn't normally engage in surf fishing, for example, with an ultra-light spinning rod, or fly fish with a casting rod blank. So first and foremost, rods and reels were the initial and typically the most substantial acquisitions within an angler's arsenal. That often became an intimidating task with the considerable number of rod types and reel models in the marketplace, and has only gotten more daunting with more targeted fishing tools like artificial smart baits. In the current recreational fishing landscape anglers now make rod and reel buying decisions very often predicated on the particular lures they intend to use. One of the market segments where this is most obvious is with freshwater bass. Anglers who fish for both largemouth and smallmouth bass frequently rig multiple outfits to match the artificial bait of choice and for any given situation. This gives them the advantage of being able to grab a suitable pre-rigged outfit as the situation requires without having to re-rig a rod and reel each time the angler chooses to change a bait. This form of fishing requires individual rods matched to the artificial bait being used to maximize that bait's potential. In a sense, modern manufacturers reverse-engineer rods to match the attributes of the smart baits that the angler uses. In most instances, these are specialty rods—one blank design to one specific bait. The folks at Temple Fork Outfitters, manufacturers of TFO rods, refer to this rod design as "technique specific action." This innovative approach exemplifies how the emerging world of smart baits influences the way in which rod manufacturers engineer and fabricate their rod blanks.

Fishing rods are becoming more specialized to meet the needs of specific fishing conditions and specific artificial baits.

The essence of a rod's ability to match effectively with an artificial hard or soft bait lies in the rod blank's degree of bend, also known as the rod's action. Fundamentally, there are three broad categories of actions: fast, medium, and slow. Rods with fast actions will exhibit a bend within the top third of the blank. This action is also sometimes referred to as a top-flex. A medium-action rod is built on a blank that flexes to a greater extent than the top-flex and bends within approximately the top first half section of the rod. This action is also often expressed as being mid-flex. And the third general type of rod action is the slow bend, or slow-flex. This action is evident in the lower third of the rod and continues well into the rod handle. Although this concept has been applied to both TFO freshwater and saltwater rods, their line of freshwater bass rods really drives home the concept of rods being designed for the express purpose of fishing specific artificial baits. Contained within the spectrum of their rod offerings are five categories of action that include: Pitching, Crankbait, Bass & Signature, Swimbait, and Drop Shot. If we take a look at each of these actions we can see how they individually and collectively work to form a system of rods that are capable of fishing many diverse baits and performing efficiently under varied fishing conditions.

TFO TECHNIQUE SPECIFIC ACTIONS
Pitching

This blank design utilizes a very fast, stiff tip that facilitates greater accuracy when using the pitching style of casting to propel heavier artificials like jigs, heavy baits, and weighted plastics. The stiffer action of these rods also aids in quick and powerful hook sets.

Crankbait

The crankbait action is softer than the pitching blank. This enables a more even loading of the blank from the butt to the tip. This degree of bend enhances the swimming motion of diving baits with wide bills. This action also supports distance casting and solid hook sets.

Bass & Signature

This design yields a mid-range action, loading from the tip and bending progressively to a more stiff action. A rod of this type is suitable for a wider range of baits and fishing methods. In many respects the mid-flexing capabilities of this blank make it very versatile and capable of effectively handling a wide range of artificial baits.

Swimbait

This action is defined by a soft tip section combined with a robust butt section. The softer tip makes it easier to cast heavier lures greater distances, while a strong butt section aids in the effective retrieval of swimbaits, and in setting the hook.

Drop Shot

The Drop Shot rod features a soft tip action, enabling the angler to detect subtle strikes that result from the use of finesse baits. This action is also efficient for making shorter casts and delivering those casts with more precise lure placement.

Anglers can achieve an even greater degree of rod utility by varying the length of the rod blank, allowing a broader array of lures. For example, if we look at the TFO Bass & Signature rods, the action of a 6'-9" length rod is an excellent choice for skipping baits into and around visible structure and obstacles, while the action in the 7'-3" length rod is ideal for baits like tube baits, plastic worms, and lipless crank baits, among other artificial lures. Furthermore, rodmakers build on blanks that run the gamut from ultra light to extra heavy, with many categories in between. The TFO power ratings are an example of that for both their conventional and spinning rods. A power rating expresses a rod blank's intrinsic resistance to bending or stiffness. When one combines the potential of mixing and matching the variables of rod length, action, and power rating, it is easy to see how diverse modern rods can be, and how they have a defined capability to handle a wide range of contemporary smart baits.

While conventional and spinning rods have undergone some of the most beneficially progressive changes to meet the demands of anglers who fish hi-tech artificial baits, fly rods have also continued to transform as science, engineering, and design techniques have evolved. Although hand-crafted bamboo rods are still very much in demand primarily among trout anglers, and fiberglass rods are witnessing a revival of sorts among some segments of the recreational fishing industry, other rod-building materials currently dominate the fly fishing market. The most common materials in modern fly rods are high modulus carbon/graphite, boron/composites, as well as titanium/graphite combinations. What these space-age fibers offer is significantly improved strength, greater power, and lightness. Fly rod design has also become quite diverse, especially with the advent of specialty fishing

High technology fly rods are capable of handling the toughest of offshore game fish

and the rapid growth of saltwater fly fishing. New materials and techniques have allowed fly tiers to create exceptionally-large and effectively-designed flies that swim like real prey fish when retrieved, and these require new tapers and rod designs to handle these new extra-large flies. Air resistance and some additional drag during the retrieve from those larger flies have set the criteria for new taper designs for these flies. This has resulted in stiffer, faster, and stouter tip actions, as well as shorter rods that deliver more punch.

Rick Pope, Chairman of Temple Fork Outfitters/TFO Rods, offers some insights into the continued evolution of fly rods: "The next generation will be a function of both engineering and materials advances. Gary Loomis's great quote that 'weight is a detriment to performance' continues to be the driving force for most all rod (blank) builders. Energy that is used in stabilizing the blank is obviously wasted relative to what is stored in the blank when the caster bends (loads) the rod and then stops (unloads) the rod in order to generate maximum line or lure speed. The compromise is that most all lighter weight materials sacrifice durability . . . and thus engineering is challenged to optimize these two key elements in rod performance." The TFO Rod Performance Matrix puts into perspective the end result of an engineering process that produces strong, versatile, and lighter rods. The "matrix" is in essence a formula that balances three key elements of how fly rods perform: presentation, distance, and lifting. The best way to look at this matrix is through the extremes at opposite ends of the fly-fishing spectrum.

In the first instance, let's examine a trout angler fishing size 20 midges for small, wary spring creek trout. Of utmost importance to that angler is a rod's ability to deliver a small fly with finesse, so presentation is the critical element. Distance is of secondary importance and, for all practical purposes, lifting power minimized in this instance. Now let's flip to the complete opposite end of the matrix formula and focus on an angler fly fishing for mako sharks. Distance is not a critical factor, especially if one is fishing from a boat and chumming sharks to move up a slick where they are visible to the angler, often within close proximity of the boat. In this scenario presentation plays a secondary role since delicate casting is not an issue. If anything, the more noise the large, bulky fly makes when hitting the water the better, since sharks are curious creatures and will seek out the source of the sound. Yet the rod must be capable of delivering a very large fly. Once a shark is hooked, the critical element the matrix equation becomes lifting power and strength to subdue a large marine fish. So with respect to of shark fishing the order of importance of the matrix elements is: power, presentation, and then distance.

A personal example that immediately comes to mind with fly fishing for sharks occurred not with a mako but rather with a very large and stubborn blue shark. The big blue had come right up the chum slick and circled the boat, at times close enough to touch it. It was a hot fish and very receptive to eating a fly. After finally realizing that it was hooked, the shark dove for the bottom, which was 129 feet. My fishing companions watched as the electronics revealed the shark's descent. They kidded that they'd be taking a lunch break while I fought the shark. At that moment, I failed to see the humor in the situation. The fish reached the bottom and hung there for what seemed like an eternity, but was more like thirty minutes. I attempted on several occasions to try and move the fish up but hadn't put the full potential of the rod behind my lifts. So the shark lingered at the twenty fathoms mark. After forty-five minutes of give and take and give back, I was beginning to feel as if this blue shark was going to get the better of me. I was fishing with a TFO Bluewater 13–15-weight rod and decided that I would go for broke and give that shark all that this rod could offer. I lifted deep from the butt section so as to engage the action of the entire rod and I felt the shark move. I regained six inches of line and the fish did not drop back. At that point I felt that I had him. I lifted again, followed by another six-inch recovery of line. And then another six inches, and another, and finally the fish began to move back up the water column, where I regained even more line back onto the reel spool. After all was said and done we removed the fly from the jaws of an approximately 170-pound blue shark and released it to challenge another angler. The lifting power of the rod blank was the only reason we were ultimately able to subdue that shark.

Cliff Pace is a professional bass angler who won the highly-coveted Bass Master Classic in 2013. Pace has fished in five "classics" and has placed in the top ten in twenty-six other tournaments. There is no doubt that Cliff has an extraordinary comprehension of bass fishing. He is a student of the game and works to continually improve his tournament performances, his knowledge of black bass, and his mastery of tackle and associated gear. I had an opportunity to talk with Cliff about this book and about the impact of science and technology on both tournament fishing and recreational fishing. His insights shed some interesting light on this subject. In Pace's experience:

"Every aspect of fishing has been influenced by technology. Electronics have obviously benefitted from technology and science, but to a great extent so have rods, reels, artificial baits, and lines. As technology evolves and improves, its impact upon professional and recreational fishing will likewise benefit." Pace places great emphasis on advancements in line development: "It wasn't too long ago that the only line choice that anglers had was mono-filament, but that has all changed. Now there are co-polymer lines, fluoro-carbon lines, hybrid lines, and braid. And lines have had a direct influence over new rod designs." What this suggests, for example, is that the sensitivity and lack of stretch in braided lines requires a rod designed to take advantage of those attributes.

We also talked specifically about rods. Pace is a TFO rod design advisor instrumental in the development of TFO's Techniques Specific rods. According to Pace, "No one rod fits all fishing situations. Rods are designed and selected for their application, much like the club choices a golfer makes when confronted with the different challenges of each hole on a golf course. The same can be said of an angler fishing different baits under varied fishing conditions." Pace is emphatic that choice of rods is highly application driven. "When I fish crank baits I want a rod designed for crank baits. When I flip baits, I want a rod that maximizes that form of fishing. Again, it is like a golfer selecting the right club."

While modern rods can function well with various generations of reels, they perform best when matched to contemporary reels. In keeping with the theme of stronger and lighter fly rods, reels too have undergone a makeover to achieve the same end results. Reel makers have reduced excess weight, while anodized aircraft-grade aluminum has become a standard construc-tion material due to its high strength-to-weight relationship. Open-frame spools also contribute to this new-age strength-to-weight ratio. More power-ful and sealed drag systems constructed of carbon fibers or Teflon add to the overall high-tech profile of modern fly reels, achieve a smoothness to effi-ciently overcome inertias, and effectively help to subdue big fish. And those reels also create a more efficient balance of the rod and reel combination in the hands of the angler. In addition to the pure technical advancements of materials, many new-age reel enhancements also play to the modern genera-tion of smart baits. Designers are creating new reels for specific fishing applications that involve the specialized features of individual smart baits.

For example, various spinning and casting reels with high line retrieval ratios are ideal for freshwater bass anglers who rip buzzbaits, spinnerbaits, and crank baits along at high speeds. Lower retrieve ratios are also available for slower and more deliberate finesse fishing. Similarly, larger saltwater reels can now perform the high retrieve task associated with artificial lures designed and used for large offshore species like tuna. And just like their corresponding rods, reels feature qualities that facilitate various fishing methods such as with pitching, drop shots, and artificial worm fishing. Fly reels have also transformed in much the same manner, becoming lighter, stronger, and with smoother drag systems.

As technology continues to advance, those improvements will help to support the design of smarter and more effective artificial baits, as well as the equipment necessary to fish them. For all practical purposes there is no limit to the degree with which those advancements will move forward to enhance the fishing experience. In many respects those improved artificial bait designs will drive innovation of rods and reels, but the reverse will also prove true, as we have seen with the advent of braided lines. It is the smart angler who embraces change, applies that change to his or her own fishing experience, and then embarks upon a path of continual learning and improvement. One of the things that has always struck me about my own personal fishing is that just when I begin to think that I have all the bases covered with respect to certain fishing conditions and situations, the fish will blow a fastball right by me. And if I am lucky enough to figure out that pitch in time to salvage the outing and adjust my timing, then they will next throw an unhittable slider. So learning to adjust to the fishing moment is often more important than what might be attached to the end of your line. Incorporating a science and technology mindset into your fishing works to broaden the tools at your disposal and will most assuredly help to make you a better angler.

CHAPTER 14

MATCHING THE BAIT

I n 1955, Dr. Ernest Schwiebert Jr. penned the seminal volume of trout fishing and trout flies titled, *Matching the Hatch*. By 1972 the book was in its eighth printing and it has become a very popular read among serious trout anglers. In many respects the volume had become a fly-selection "bible" of sorts. The fundamental premise of the book is that the trout angler must have more than just an understanding of the trout that he or she pursues. The author proposed that successful anglers will also need a working knowledge of entomology and an understanding of the natural flies that trout eat. Only then can the angler "match the hatch" by selecting the flies that most appropriately replicate the life-cycle phase of various aquatic flies. Those flies are most notably mayflies, caddis, and stoneflies. Each phase of the flies' relatively short life spans has significant relevance to the trout angler's fly selection process. Schwiebert's writings on this subject led to an almost cult-like following among anglers who embraced the concept as a critical path to catching trout consistently. Eventually other writers followed suit, like Art Flick with his *Streamside Guide*, and before long the methodology of "matching the hatch" became a universally-accepted protocol for selecting trout flies under real-time, streamside fishing conditions. Although the origins of matching the hatch were already well-rooted in fly fishing for freshwater trout, over time the phrase became a rather generally-accepted term among anglers in the context of selecting natural or artificial baits for any given species of fish.

Regardless of where anglers fish or what they seek to catch, one of their preliminary goals is to match the prevalent bait. Many view the task of understanding bait and its seasonal movements and habits as one of the most critical elements for a consistent catch. All successful anglers, whether they fish freshwater or saltwater, spend as much time understanding the impact of bait movements, tendencies, and habits of key baitfish as they do understanding the similar traits of the fish they pursue. Bait movements and

Two seminal volumes on the art and science of matching the hatch.

behaviors will vary with the seasons, water temperature, time of day, weather, and other variables in all bodies of water, so it is the "smart" angler who keys in on those bait transition periods. In many instances the interrelationship between predator and prey is so great that the over-arching principle in most fishing situations is that if you find the bait, you find the fish.

Of equal importance is the proper selection of an artificial bait to mimic the natural bait upon which the targeted species feed. And just like Dr. Schwiebert's suggestion that the wise trout angler become somewhat of an amateur entomologist to better understand the trout's primary foods source, it can also be suggested that anglers embrace the fundamentals of ichthyology and familiarize themselves with the anatomy, life cycles, and behavioral traits of baitfish and other game fish prey. Even a familiarity of basic baitfish anatomy can go a long way toward helping anglers gain advantage. For example, in the most simplistic terms all baitfish are shaded typically in three tones of color: a dark top; a light underside; and transitioning flanks. The process of evolution and the laws of nature have allowed this shading to emerge so that when baitfish are viewed by a predator from beneath, the lighter coloration blends with the sky and light from above. When those same baitfish are viewed from above, their dark backs blend with the dark bottom and the diminishing light that occurs farther down the water column. And when viewed from the side, the blended shading and muted tones offer somewhat of a camouflaged silhouette.

For the most part, this form of body shading gives the baitfish some degree of protection from predation but, obviously, it doesn't always work to the advantage of the baitfish, otherwise predators would starve. That is why predatory fish have evolved with more sophisticated senses that can detect other aspects of the presence of a food source—sound, taste, feel, and smell all come into play when predatory fish hunt for food. As we have already seen, it is a characteristic of smart baits to appeal to those highly sensitized senses. Yet matching the bait can be a process that can go from the simple to the sublime. Some of the most successful lures and flies of all time have followed the simple rule of baitfish shading, while other, equally-productive lures have gone all out to represent every minute detail to replicate anatomical accuracy, natural coloration, and shading. When designing the most fundamental artificial baits or flies, the creator of the bait will often take this form of natural shading into account.

While replicating nature's color patterns is important when matching artificial lures to the available bait, so too are the other key features of profile, size and overall shape. At times, going against the grain when matching natural bait will produce strong results, but more often than not a precision match to size, shape, and profile will enjoy the most consistent success. There are many instances of this occurring in both fresh water and salt water. For example, when east coast striped bass feed on sand eels, the perfect artificial match, whether lure or fly, is one that has a slender profile and shape, and is as close as possible to the bait's length. Very often, simply matching those characteristics (and manipulating the bait effectively during the retrieve) will be sufficient to trigger strikes. But at other times, a more sophisticated and accurate portrayal of bait will be required. To achieve this, today's modern lure designers apply all the technology and science at their disposal to achieve some amazingly lifelike renditions of natural bait in artificial form. One such modern company that is striving to do just that is LIVETARGET. This Ontario, Canada-based company is an innovative and progressive designer and manufacturer of exceptionally lifelike hard and soft plastic baits. The founding principle of the LIVETARGET brand of lures is: " . . . to create the most

LIVETARGET lures have taken the realism school of lure design to the next level of anatomical precision.

realistic, lifelike and anatomically accurate fishing lures that 'Match-the-Hatch' to target all varieties of game fish in both freshwater and saltwater." Since its inception, LIVETARGET has produced over 750 different lures to help raise the bar on the production of contemporary smart baits. They took the original Schwiebert concept of matching the hatch in fly fishing, and transformed it into a business mission with respect to the production of modern hard and soft baits.

The effectiveness of precise replica artificials has a lot to do with the species of fish targeted and the specific circumstances and fishing conditions. It also has a lot to do with how fish get stimulated to strike. For example, let's take a look at a freshwater angler casting buzz baits or spinner baits to large-mouth bass. For all practical purposes, those two artificial lure forms don't look, smell, or taste like anything that a bass would eat. In effect, they are the antithesis of the match-the-bait concept. Although they are very effective baits, one might wonder why any fish would strike either one. The very first time I cautiously used them my expectation was that bass would flee from the contraptions rather than embrace them. While one might overthink the bass's motivation to eat such a bait, the explanation as to why is rather simple. Largemouth bass physiology is such that their method of hunting prey relies heavily on the simulation of their lateral line. This is especially true in dark, murky, and muddied waters were the sense of sight is impaired. Under these kinds of conditions a bass's lateral line becomes a primary indicator of the presence of bait, as the movements of those bait emit vibrations to the water. Those vibrations are picked up by the lateral line. Spinner baits and buzz baits make a lot of noise when retrieved and, therefore, generate a trail of vibrations in the water that a bass can detect and track as a food source. The noise of those baits also acts as an agitator to prompt reaction strikes. Although spinner baits and buzz baits can motivate strikes when water visibility is low, they are also uniquely effective in clear water. Yet again, the primary reason is the effect of sound and, in the instance of clear water, sight. Baits of this type also tend to appeal to a fish's territorial and competitive instincts. If one were to think in terms of art, this form of bait might be considered abstract.

Positioned in the middle of the spectrum are those situations where a non-precise matching of the bait is acceptable for stimulating fish to strike. That is, when matching the natural bait with an imitation of suitable size, profile, and color it is enough to get the job done. Conceptually, this method can be viewed as a form of "impressionistic" art: Giving the impression of a real live form, but not quite something that is a totally anatomically accurate rendition. Classic dry flies, plastic worms, certain generic swim baits, soft plastic artificials, and a variety of crank baits and popping plugs are examples of that bait form.

At the complete opposite end of the gamut from these somewhat abstract baits is what can be referred to as the realism school of smart baits. This category of lures strives to achieve realistic perfection when presenting artificial baits to fish. From the perspective of contemporary lure design, the realism school of smart baits embraces all that is available from modern technology and science, and the replication of minute details transferred from the natural bait to the artificial reproduction. The belief is that accurately matching all attributes and characteristics of live bait will only work to increase the effectiveness of the artificial replicas. In the case of what we have come to classify as "smart baits," this means creating a bait that appeals to specific, if not all, senses of a game fish.

As we have already discussed, predatory fish rely on their senses to find, track, and capture their food. In some instances a singular sense is the primary receptor, but all-in smart baits will be designed to appeal to all of a fish's senses or at least those that are of importance to how specific fish species feed. The ultimate smart lure to match the bait will resonate with a fish's senses of sight, sound, feel, scent, and taste. There are now lures on tackle shop shelves that feel, taste, sound, smell and look like their real counterparts. Some enterprising manufacturers are even adding electronic signatures to their baits that emit vibrations to which certain species will respond. One company has even embedded a small, hi-definition camera into its signature popper that gives the angler a fish-eye view of the actual strike. The camera signal can also be streamed to a mobile device and shared on social networks. In addition, the same manufacturer has built-in sensors that monitor such environmental factors as water temperature, water clarity, salinity, acidity, and oxygen levels. This brings the application of science to fishing lures to an entirely new level, and gives the anglers access to some critical metrics that affect fishing conditions. These designs highlight the future of innovation in the creation of next-generation smart baits.

The magic that is social media allows us all to develop and participate in communities of like-minded folks who share common interests and passions. And so it is with my contacts, most of whom have an interest in the outdoors and in fishing. While writing this chapter I asked them to describe their thought process when selecting an artificial bait to match specific baits. Taken as a whole, their responses weave an interesting and informative pattern about lure selection. Some of these folks are professionals, others are accomplished amateurs, but their thought processes inform your own method for choosing the right artificial lure to match bait. It matters not if their responses are one-liners or full paragraphs in the following angling wisdom; their experiences will help you in your lure-selection process. Whether treating the subject of hard bait, soft bait, or fly, the message is transferable from one artificial bait form to the next.

Tom Keer, renowned outdoor writer, avid angler, and upland hunter: "Match your fly color to the water color. Baitfish pick up colors and hues in their environment. A silverside over an eelgrass bed has a greenish tint, while it has a yellowish tint when it's over sand. They're dark brown, purple, and black at night. Add sunlight, their movement, and the depth in which they hold and their colors change even more. Sometimes they appear to have purple hues while other times they carry a purple coloration. All other baitfish are that way, too, but don't take my word for it. Instead, grab a mask and a snorkel, hit the water, and see for yourself. You'll be amazed that you don't see a dominant silver lateral line on a silverside as you do when they're in your hand. You'll also have the answer to that burning question: Why did the lemon and yellow pattern slam 'em on a flat in bright sunlight, and then shut off when a cloud cover rolled in? The coloration of the environment changed, and so did the baitfish. Put on a pattern with more greens, lavender, and purple and you'll start catching 'em up. You catch what you are, so if you want to catch fish, be the fish. Small, aggressive fish will hit chartreuse flies stripped at very fast speeds. If you're after schoolies, that approach will work just fine. But if you're after bigger fish then you have to think like a bigger fish. Show them what they're used to seeing by matching your fly to the water color and you'll hook them regularly and consistently."

Bob Veverka, accomplished fly angler, fly tier, and book author: "Size, shape, and color, length of fly is most important, as is the retrieve of the fly. Sometimes it's the fly, other times the way you retrieve the fly."

Steve Piatt, *outdoor news* editor, outdoor writer, accomplished angler and hunter: "I'm constantly amazed at some of the realistic, replica fly tiers and their work that appears lifelike. But I often wonder, is that what the trout sees when it's looking up? That's why I've always been a disciple of the late Gary LaFontaine, who spent countless hours under water, researching a trout's reaction to various patterns. Size matters as well, as does color. But myself? When I'm about ready to beat my head against the rock wondering what a trout is taking, I'm reminded of what a western guide said when one of his clients asked that question. His response? A drag-free drift."

Eric Fieldstat, recreational and competitive bass angler: "As an avid freshwater bass angler, my favorite lure is a jig with a pork or plastic trailer, a.k.a. Jig 'n' Pig. There isn't a pond, lake, or river anywhere that doesn't have crawfish as a primary forage for largemouth and smallmouth, which this lure represents. I like to say that any color jig is good as long as it is black/blue but I will also throw green or brown jigs depending on sun and cloud conditions. Size ranges from $^3/_{16}$–1 oz. according to depth and the structure I'm fishing. That also determines whether I use a spinning or bait casting outfit with anywhere from six- to sixty-pound test line. The jig is a very weedless bait that can be fished deep or shallow and can be thrown into any heavy cover such as weeds, rocks, trees, pads, and docks where bass are found. I don't leave home without this versatile lure."

Bob Popovics, world-renowned fly angler and fly innovator: "Don't always change your fly first, change your presentation."

Bill Elliott, accomplished international angler, trout fishing expert, and renowned sporting artist: "If I had to give but one piece of advice to an angler just starting out, it would be never stop learning about the species of fish you are targeting. Each species has a tell that you should identify and then design the lure of fly that best represents that instinct to feed."

Captain Brian Horsley, Outer Banks Fly Fishing: "Matching the hatch to a point works, but to me presentation is as important."

Captain Greg Myerson, current striped bass world record holder, founder, owner, and CEO of The World Record Striper Company: "Attenuation loss, that is the loss of colors underwater, is most important. At a depth of fifteen feet red disappears; at twenty-five feet orange disappears; at forty feet yellow; at seventy feet green. It works the same horizontally as well. So as you go deeper or as it gets dark you need darker colors to be more visible to the fish. It's like looking through fog for something: If it's white it's harder to see than black."

Laura Pisano, recreational fly angler, Italy: "Size matters, but the fly has to be fished properly. Water conditions are also important like color, clarity, and wave activity. If baits are small but I can't properly work a small fly due to water conditions, I change. Sometimes I do not match the bait at all, and that can be a solution as well. When fishing from the boat, bait size and the depth is important. Color is not as important in my choice."

Dennis Zambrotta, recreational angler and accomplished surf caster: "Ninety percent of the time a surfcaster's presentation is within one foot of the water's surface, while striped bass spend a majority of their existence within two feet of the bottom. Get deeper."

Captain David Blinken, North Flats Guiding: "Presentation is paramount when sight fishing. Having a fly that doesn't make too much of a commotion on the water in quiet situations is also something to consider. Finally, approach is important so weary fish are not spooked. I find sparsely-tied flies work best in my local waters and matching either bait or the hues of the environment in which they are used. Depending on species and location one needs to be open to other patterns when not fishing familiar waters."

Captain Tom Mikoleski, Grand Slam Charters: "Old standby 'matching the hatch' will rarely let one down. Figure out what the game fish are feeding on and try to match size, color, and action. On the rare cases that doesn't get one a bite, shift gears and try live bait."

Nancy Hopping, guide, fly angler, fly tier, outdoor photographer: "For me, it is all in the presentation and believing in your fly. It comes down to confidence. I can use one fly and catch stripers and use that same fly for freshwater trout, salmon, bass, and bluegill."

Walter Koda, avid recreational angler: "To me the key to success in catching fish whether fly fishing or using lures has to be size, color, and presentation. This goes along with matching the hatch or sizing the lure to the bait the fish are targeting. When all three are used together your chances of hooking up are dramatically increased. This holds true for all species of fish."

Captain Paul Dixon, Fly Fishing Montauk: "The fly is often not the problem; it's current. Fish don't feed 24-7. If the current isn't moving and fish aren't feeding it won't matter what fly you use. We see this demonstrated on the flats a lot. Fish refuse the fly at dead tide and then hammer the same fly repeatedly when water starts to move. If I know I have good tide and moving water, then I will change the fly and try to match what baits I think are around. Then I work on presentation and different strips."

Captain Terry Nugent, Riptide Charters: "I always try to match the hatch while being different. Match shape and color, but be slightly larger. Match size, shape, and color, but make surface disturbance. Be the same while standing out."

Michael Rioles, avid recreational angler: "In freshwater, I like to see what they are eating and then match the size and color of the fly that the fish are keyed in on. Presentation is also key in freshwater to trigger a bite. In salt water I like my fly to be a little bigger than what they are eating, and I feel like that will make it stick out better from the rest. Like people, some fish want the biggest meal they can get for their efforts. Color and shape are also important but not as much depending on the fish we are chasing. Presentation in salt water, I feel is not as important but it does depend on which fish we are chasing."

Capt. Thomas Cornicelli, Back Bay Outfitters: "Complex olfactory is not to be overlooked. Striped bass smell thousands of times better than humans, as well as many land animals. With that being said, I fished deepwater channels of course for large bass with sinking lines and big flies. My approach and strategy: The fly has to be weighted for both casting and to track perfectly through the water column on the retrieve . . . and well designed. Keeping in mind this game fish's acute sense of smell, a steady retrieve is not going to cut it for these larger fish. My success comes from an extremely fast, rapid-fire retrieve 95 percent of the time."

Rich Zaleski, guide, outdoor writer/blogger, and accomplished freshwater and saltwater angler: "Nine times out of ten, running depth and size are far more important than color. From a largemouth bass perspective, don't get carried away with color. Except when chasing a school of baitfish in open water, they are opportunistic feeders and are perfectly willing to try to eat the next potential meal that comes within range, whatever it is."

Captain Sandy Noyes, Rumrunner Guide Service: "Since we fish mostly in strong currents and rips, presentation is not a big factor. Size and shape of the baitfish is more important. I have found that matching the hatch color-wise is not always important. My most productive squid fly is banana yellow. For albies, there are two rips about ten miles apart. In one, they like a tan and white deceiver. In the other it's turquoise and white. If you switch colors they don't work. Sometimes you just need to experiment a little."

Steven Thomas, owner at Only on the Fly: "I find that flies that have a more natural color usually outproduce something gaudy and too flashy. The real key is to have the fly appear wounded. Remember, wounded prey is always singled out by predators."

David Legg, ardent recreational angler: "I like to see how a lure behaves right when I stop the retrieve. Does it drop, rest, pop up like cork? Does it list badly? I like to see it resemble the behavior of the bait it mimics. It's a critical strike point for any lure."

Bob Clouser, world-renowned angler, fly innovator, and creator of the Clouser Deep Minnow: "For smallmouth bass on the rivers I fish it can be color, conditions, depth, and/or presentation that will make the difference."

Captain Gary Dubiel, owner, Spec Fever Guide Service: "Getting the fly or lure to the fish is more important than the fly or color. Adding weight in the fly or line and allowing it to get down to the fish increases the odds in your favor."

Captain John Luchka, Long Run Fishing charters: "For me, in shallow back bays in the early spring for stripers, I like using a popping cork with a nice rattle to it, and for below, based on the water depth, I'll use an olive-over-white Clouser soaked in a scent like bloodworm or even menhaden oil to help the bass locate the scent trail, and also via the sound of the popping cork. Very similar to how they catch redfish in murky waters down south. As many of our backbay waters are murky, this is a great search bait and a proven producer. You can also use a small, soft bait like Gulp! minnow versus a fly. Used on light spincasting outfits you can cover a lot of water while also being stealthy."

Bob Lindquist, distinguished fly tier/innovator: "Critical factors determining fly selection are where in the water column is the fly best placed, the water conditions, and then casting conditions, what is best to capture the fish's attention: Is imitation or attraction best, is it imitation of action or imitation of appearance? And finally, how can I present this fly so as to take advantage of the inherent qualities of the fly that determined my choice?"

Kevin Arculeo, fly innovator: "The right size gets you the prize."

Lee Weil, all-around outdoorswoman, fly angler, and fly tier: "I believe the action of the fly or lure is the most important factor that triggers strikes. That's why I 'test drive' my new patterns until they move naturally in the water. Materials can be changed and weight can be applied to different areas of the shank to change the way a fly swims. I love tweaking the flies and getting results."

CHAPTER 15

HOW IT ALL COMES TOGETHER

As I thought about everything presented in this book thus far, I pondered how to best tie each of the pieces together to illustrate how smart baits can work best for anglers. After considering a whole host of possibilities, I settled on one unique set of experiences that I have had fishing for sharks. As one of the most highly-evolved fish species in the world's oceans, sharks have often been referred to as perfect predators. The primary reason for this designation is that sharks benefit from a network of acute senses that work in concert to locate and home in on sources of food. As apex marauders, sharks depend heavily on their abilities to outmaneuver and outsmart their prey. Successful shark anglers employ a wide range of techniques and devices that appeal to all of a shark's senses in order to get them to strike. The more those senses can be collectively stimulated, the better are the chances for a strike. While anglers conduct most shark fishing in a traditional fashion with natural baits spread out at different depths within the water column, my brand of sharking is done with feathers in the form of oversized and gaudy flies.

The first time I mentioned flies and sharks in the same sentence to conventional offshore anglers, the disbelieving, eye rolling, and head-shaking response was an emphatic, "There's no *bleeping* way you can do that." The concept almost sounds counterintuitive: Carnivorous predators eating feathers! But feeding flies to oceanic apex predators is not only possible, the process itself offers some of the most exciting and consistent big game fly fishing to be had. And much of that potential has a lot to do with how "smarter" artificial baits like modern flies in tandem with other methods and techniques can tempt a large, traditionally meat-consuming fish to eat a fake bait. One of my first experiences with feeding feathers to sharks, and a number of subsequent outings, began to solidify for me the need to think

Apex predators like sharks respond well to the stimulation of all their feeding senses.

differently and more expansively about how one can motivate fish by appealing to their network of senses.

I had joined with a friend for an offshore outing. He and I shared a similar interest in catching sharks on flies, and our goal for the day was to try our luck at getting a mako shark to eat one of my fly patterns. We traveled to an area that had been active with sharks and set up a traditional chum slick. The goal when presenting flies to sharks is to get them close to the boat by getting them to following a chum slick back "upstream" to the source of the chum. With this phase of the game anglers appeal to a shark's very acute sense of smell. In addition to the chum bag that emitted a steady stream of food particles into the water, we had also butterflied large menhaden and mackerel and hung them over the downstream side of the boat. That tactic very much enhanced the amount and intensity of scent in the water. Sharks are also curious creatures and once their olfactory system is aroused they will seek out the origins of the food they smell. That, hopefully, brings them to the chum bag and within distance of a fly cast.

Once we had a good scent slick underway, my fishing partner opened one of the storage hatches and retrieved an electrical device known as a Mako Magnet. This vibrating apparatus makes sounds that replicate those made by wounded bait, and thus indicate an easy meal. Sharks have a network of electro-receptor cells along their snouts that are called the ampullae de

Lorenzini. These cells aid sharks in sensing electric and magnetic fields. While the sophistication of the "ampullae" help sharks to find potential food through the electric signatures that bait gives off, those receptor cells are very sensitive to the electric signals given off by devices like the mako magnet. Successful shark anglers I know swear by the "magnets," and some have offered the advice that the device be protected when submerged in water, because sharks will attempt to eat it. One angler that I know has gotten very creative with the method he employs to attract sound. He puts a vibrator in a condom, and submerges it in the chum bucket. I can say from personal experience fishing with this guy, that he attracts and catches some huge sharks. This trick certainly highlights that within the wide world of fishing, innovation and creativity are indeed the parents of invention.

At this point in the game, our mako-attracting efforts included tactics that would appeal to the shark's sense of smell, an ability to detect electric signals, and its sense of hearing sounds in water. My oversized fly, which could be described as a chicken on a hook, would also appeal to any curious mako's senses of vision, smell, and hearing. Flies for sharks are first and foremost full of stimulating colors that the fish find tempting. The fly had tied on was a combination of red, yellow, hot orange, and fluorescent chartreuse. It also contained a small scent pocket that I saturated with a blend of bunker and mackerel oils. For good measure I rubbed some of the oil mixture on the feathers of the fly. This would offer a somewhat natural taste when the shark ate the fly. I affixed glass cylinder containing small beads to the body of the fly during the tying process to create an auditory rattling effect. We had most of the sensory bases covered, so any shark that ventured up the chum slick would be bombarded with a veritable rainstorm of stimuli. Our efforts now became a waiting game. Some days you wait for hours, and other days things happen fast. Well, we didn't have to wait long to watch a hydrodynamic short fin mako zip through the chum slick just yards from the boat. The fish came in hot and we could tell by its attitude that is wanted to eat. I grabbed the fly rod and made a cast, allowing the fly to dead drift among the floating pieces of chum.

No sooner had the fly hit the water when the big fish turned on it. I saw the take and strip set several times, simultaneously lifting the stout fly rod to set the hook. At first, the fish had no idea it was hooked. I would suppose this was the first time the apex predator had grabbed a bunch of feathers and found itself attached to the end of a fly line that was annoyingly impeding its progress. It swam off leisurely, behaving as if the fly was just a minor annoyance stuck in its jaw. I set the hook yet again, and that time the fish responded. The mako took off at a pace that would have made a sprinter look like he was standing still in the Olympic 100 meter finals; and that was just for openers. The first straightaway run was at such a blistering pace it had me wondering if I had enough backing on the fly reel to get through the first impressive dash. The reel's drag was mashed down yet backing literally poured off the spool. Suddenly, the mako went ballistic. The shark blasted from the water like a sub-surface to air missile, cart-wheeling to a height that seemed surreal. I let out with a roar of joy and bowed to mako, just like one does to a tarpon on a fly rod, but the fish was no longer where the tip of my rod pointed. In a heartbeat, it surfaced again seventy-yards diagonally from the position of its first jump. It is no wonder these fish can catch speedy tuna. The word fast in this context is an understatement. Half a dozen more similar jumps and long runs had me jogging around the inside of the boat holding tight to the tenuous connection that hooked me to a tenacious and determined quarry. The intense runs, jumps, and constant pressure from a heavy-duty fly stick all worked to help tire the shark. Finally, I had gained backing and then fly line onto the reel. It was with great satisfaction and elation that I watched as a friend grabbed the leader and prepared to deploy the release stick. As the mako swam off all I could say was, "Wow! that was amazing!" I learned a lot of lessons from that mako shark about integrating the elements that motivated the fish to strike. But one other shark fly-fishing experience highlights just how alluring a smarter artificial bait can be.

I was invited by a friend to accompany him on an offshore fishing trip for tuna and sharks. The tuna turned out to be uncooperative that day, so we headed back inshore to set up a chum slick. Although this was to be a traditional shark fishing outing with bait, I never leave home without stowing away at least one fly rod. When fishing for sharks using conventional methods, anglers will place a number of baits at varying depths and distances from the boat, for example, thirty, sixty, and ninety feet deep. Sharks typically eat those baits without ever revealing their presence. Within short order we had a good chum slick going with an ideal drift. The crew had rigged and placed all the natural baits out, and it was then time to wait. And wait we did, for hours without any shark activity whatsoever.

Time was beginning run out on our fishing day when one of the crew-members yelled, "Shark!" The fish was making its way up the slick and had reached the balloon marker for the bait that was set ninety feet down. We all watched as the blue shark circled the area of that bait and then disappeared. We all expected the shark to eat that bait but it didn't. Within minutes the shark reappeared at the bait suspended down at sixty feet. The fish circled that bait and then vanished yet again. Two different baits at two different depths were totally ignored. But that wasn't the end of it; the shark wasn't done tormenting us. A fin then appeared in the vicinity of the closest bait that hung at depth of thirty feet. The same scenario unfolded. The shark circled that bait, disappeared, and refused that offering.

We all scratched our heads. It was not only odd that the blue shark rejected the baits positioned at different levels of the water column, but even more confounding that the fish rejected several different types of natural bait: bluefish, bunker, and mackerel. As we waited the shark's next move, I decided to rig my fly rod just in case an up-close and-personal opportunity presented itself to get off a cast. By this time, the collective patience of the crew was

Flies designed for sharks should contain colors that can trigger reaction strikes.

wearing thin and talk had begun of reeling in the baits and calling it a day. Out of some habitual need to cast I tossed my fly into the slick. Well . . . to this day, the crew still talks about what happened next. No sooner had the fly entered the water and sunk to a level of about two feet, when that shark appeared out from the dark depths to eat it. We watched in amazement as the big maw of that fish opened and engulfed the fly.

I fought, landed, and successfully released the fish. But the questions lingered: Why did that shark pass up three of its favorite natural food sources only to eat a red, white, yellow, orange, and chartreuse amalgamation of feathers? To be candid, I have no answer. I've talked with shark experts and seasoned shark anglers and the answer still eludes me. Yet, I can offer a hypothesis. Despite their reputation and popular belief, sharks are not wanton and gluttonous killers that feed constantly. Research has shown that most sharks need a daily consumption of food that equated to about a half of a percent to three percent of their body weight. If you do the math, a 150-pound shark might eat a maximum of four and a half pounds of food a day. Compare that to a 150-pound man who consumes a hearty breakfast, lunch and dinner. Also, it is possible for a shark to eat but two suitable meals a week. That said, I suspect that the shark which passed up our natural baits had recently fed, was satiated and in a non-feeding, passive state. Then what motivated it to eat a fly?

Fish don't always strike an artificial bait out of a need to feed. As we have seen in previous chapters, there are many other factors that contribute to an strike response. Obviously, hunger is at the top of the list, but fish will strike a lure if competition from other fish is a motivator. It is sort of like, I will get to eat it first. Fish will also hit a bait for territorial reasons, as will a largemouth bass will when it protects a spawning bed, or a king salmon will when a Dolly Varden invades its red to eat the eggs. Furthermore, an artificial bait can stimulate a reaction strike by appealing to a fish's curiosity, causing an annoyance, or otherwise simply getting in its way, as is often the case with migrating and soon-to-spawn Pacific salmon. But in the case of the shark eating the fly while passing up a real-food meal, I believe the answer lies in how the hierarchy of senses is deployed. We've established a belief that the shark was not actively feeding, but when it came into contact with a big, gaudy fly that moved water, made noise, emitted scent, and stood out from among the pieces of chum, its network of senses were most likely aroused, which fueled a reaction strike. It is also quite possible that the shark's curiosity got the better of it and it simply had to sample the foreign and unknown fly to determine if it was food. That combination of scenarios paints a picture of how modern smart artificial baits target a fish's physiology and excite the senses resulting in a response. Whether the angler uses hard plastic baits, soft plastic baits, tins, jigs, or flies, the smarter a bait can be, the better the outcome.

CHAPTER 16

THE ELECTRONIC EDGE AND THE DIGITAL WORLD

I once watched a cable television show that dealt with the subject of ancient civilizations and their use of what can only be described as advanced technology. While debate may go around and around about the origins of crop circles or how the pyramids were actually built, there is some supporting evidence that validates the proposition that the ancients did indeed have and utilize forms of technology that were considered sophisticated for the time. One such example is the Parthian Battery, also known as the Baghdad Battery. It is hypothesized by some that the "battery" generated low levels of electric current that may have been used to electroplate statues with gold. A ceramic pot, a copper tube, and an iron rod comprise the device, which dates to a period between 150 BCE and 223 AD. As the theory goes, some researchers contend that an acidic liquid like lemon juice, vinegar, or grape juice interacted with the copper tube and the iron rod to produce very low levels of electric current. Over the years, a number of experiments using similar components and designs have been successful at generating small electric currents. Regardless of the actual purpose of the Parthian Battery, the fact remains that civilizations have been trying to improve their quality of life for eons and advancements in technology have been at the core of that goal.

Modern anglers seek to use technology in more ways than just with the manufacture of rods, reels and baits. Many significant and industry-changing innovations have come from the electronics segment of the industry. While I am not a dinosaur yet, I can recall a time when many anglers determined the bottom depth of a lake by lowering a weighted line to the bottom and read the depth marks that were placed at various intervals on the line, usually a foot apart. It may have been a primitive depth finder but it worked well. And if your "feel" for the bottom got to be really good, one could distinguish between various bottom structure and configurations: rocks, mud, timber, grass, etc. We used one other very low-tech gadget used back then, fitted to a length of rope that was marked with intervals of depth. But this setup used a thermometer to test the water temperatures at various depths. If my memory serves me correctly, the device I used was marketed as a Depth-O-Therm. It was simply weighted to gauge the water temperate at different depths. Although this was a really primitive piece of equipment I do recall using it on one freshwater largemouth bass trip in the early 1970s that had a very positive outcome. That simple contrivance helped me locate the preferred comfort zone of 68 to 72 degrees Fahrenheit in a reasonably large body of water on Long Island, New York. That particular area of the lake yielded two limits of bass that day which ranged from 3.5 to 5.75 pounds. Further along in my development as a bass angler I acquired an early-generation Humminbird brand fish finder. This portable, battery-operated "flasher" unit was called the Tom Mann Bird Trap. Its operation was quite simple. Once turned on, a flashing signal rotated around a circular and stationary face that was marked with depth indicators. The flashing would become more intense and highlight the depth from the return signal received from the transducer. One additional control knob allowed the angler to adjust intensity and definition of the signal. Should bait or fish be detected between the surface of the water and the bottom, additional flashes would indicate where in the water column those fish were under the boat. With some practice and a bit of trial and error, one could further interpret the size, intensity, and position of the flashes more accurately. It was, all in all, a very simple but effective fish finder.

My most memorable Bird Trap experience took place during a local bass tournament. Toward the end of that competition, my partner and I decided to fish the remaining time along a submerged weed bed in relatively deep water. Over the years, and without the aid of electronics, we had caught bass from that location sporadically and when we were lucky enough to make the right drift over the grass. But for this drift I had the flasher at the ready. We made a couple of passes in the general vicinity of the weed bed and then located the deeper edge of the grass. The flashers transmitted a "soft" signal with some depth to it and that typically indicated a grass-like bottom. We held in that area and with the aid of the trolling motor moved back and forth across that deep edge. And then at one point the flasher began to emit signals consistent with fish holding very close to the bottom. I threw out an old-school orange marker float and backed the boat off that spot. We then began casting plastic worms rigged Texas-style; it didn't take long for the first hookup. Time was running out pretty quick, but that spot yielded enough bass to take first place in the tournament. The Bird Trap had come through in the clutch.

Technology has come a very long way since the days of my portable fish finder. As a matter of fact, modern fish-finding electronics are so good I often feel that the fish don't stand a chance against a knowledgeable angler armed with state-of-the art electronics and modern smart baits. But yet again, it is the smart angler that will embrace the technology and fully utilize the tools at his or her disposal. I have a very good friend who is an excellent angler and charter boat captain. I often kiddingly refer to him as Captain Gadget, because in some respects he loves technology and new toys almost as much as he loves fishing. I don't think there's been a time that I have been on his boat when he has not proudly displayed some form of updated and upgraded electronic gadget. As a matter of fact, as I write this paragraph, Captain Gadget emailed me that "New electronics are on the way." Over the years, I have upgraded my own electronic gear, but since I am fundamentally an inshore, shallow water, and sight-fishing kind of guy, I really don't need the level of equipment that offshore or tournament anglers use. Don't get me wrong, my newest CHIRP/GPS combination fish finder is a mountain range

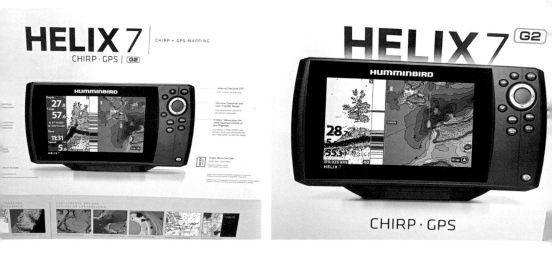

New sonar technology like CHIRP can be an indispensible tool for the boating angler.

above my first portable device, and it is a valuable piece of gear for many reasons, not the least of which is finding fish and for safety while on the water. But folks like Captain Gadget are in another league altogether. Not only do their consoles resemble a NASA control station, they seek out the very best and most current gear because smart electronics can help the angler achieve the high potential that is inherent in all modern smart baits.

Captain Gadget in real life is Captain Adrian Mason. He is the owner of Time Flies Fishing Charters and actively fishes both inshore and offshore water. His views regarding the use of contemporary electronics are quite informative and insightful. Here's a peek into Captain Mason's thinking:

> Modern technology has provided us with some of the best marine electronics we could have ever dreamed of, from forward-scan imaging to radar capable of picking up feeding birds 24 miles away. Anyone who has been on my boat will see that I love gadgets and electronics. I currently run Simrad NSS EVO2 units with down scan, side scan, and CHIRP technology. These tools have made finding fishable area much easier than we were used to. Couple that with the latest charts and maps from companies like C-Map and Navionics, you can find structure in any body of water. Not only have these electronic devices surpassed my own imagination, but they perform exceptionally well. Here's a great example of how I use these new Simrad units. If I'm fishing in a new area, I can use my side scan image transducer to provide me an MRI-looking picture of the bottom, which will reveal rock piles and bottom contours that look promising. I have the ability to use the touch screen and actually enter waypoints right on the structure I'm looking at. If I miss it, I can drag the screen backwards to find the piece I was looking for. From there I will come back with my CHIRP sonar and actually see if there are fish holding in that area. The CHIRP is so sensitive, you can see the difference between a school of baitfish and the larger fish preying on them. While no amount of electronics can make a fish eat your bait, not yet anyway, knowing where the fish are holding if more than half the battle. The rest is up to the angler to figure out and land that big one.

Contemporary fishing electronics are certainly wonders of the modern age. While it took time to interpret the flashes that appeared on the screen of my little red box, there is no mistaking what appears on the screens of modern fish finders. Flashes now look like fish, and bottom structure and contours mirror the real thing, almost always in 3D and living color. It is quite amazing to be able to mark fish and then watch as those marks approach a descending lure. And then, almost like a particular video game, one digital signature merges with the other: Fish on! But this is only the beginning of modern "fish-finder" potential. GPS capabilities, mapping, side imaging, and CHIRP (compressed high impact radar pulse) are all available to offer the best fishing-electronics experience when on the water. But the fact is that even the most rudimentary of modern fish finder/sonar units on the market now provide information that is in many ways superior to higher-end models of only a decade ago. For many anglers, the basic depth and fish location capabilities are really all that they need, but if you want to fly on the edge of available technology, it is there for the taking. Let's examine what forms of electronics can elevate the angler's overall "smart" fishing.

GLOBAL POSITIONING SYSTEM

The integration of GPS into most sonar and fish finder devices is fairly common these days even with some of the entry-level units. GPS is fundamentally a global positioning system that utilizes satellites to determine location anywhere in the world. It operates independently of any other forms of data transmission networks like cell phones, the Internet, or digital cable. While originally developed for military purposes in the 1970s and 1980s, it soon became apparent that the private and civilian sectors could also benefit greatly from this technology, and in 1996 President Clinton signed a directive to allow for GPS technology to be used for both military and civilian use. Subsequent to that, in 1998 the administration further implemented policy and plans to upgrade the quality of signals for civilian use, enabling a higher degree of positioning accuracy. By the year 2000 civilian-use GPS could provide a higher degree of positioning accuracy. Today, GPS use is so common that one would be hard pressed to find a new automobile without one. Even those folks who drive older vehicles are very likely to have portable GPS devices affixed to their dashboards or consoles. The same is true of those whose playground is the water. Virtually all sonar and fish finder manufacturers offer models that include built-in GPS capabilities. The significance of this is apparent to the boating angler, in freshwater or saltwater. The benefits of GPS to the angler include being able to navigate to and return from a long trip on the most efficient course, mark and save favorite fishing spots, chart a course, and save way points. When combined with a sonar/fish finding unit, the GPS can instantly save the coordinates for a productive fishing location, or one that may have future potential. And one enterprising company has developed a product that uses GPS to allow a boater to locate and automatically maintain an anchoring position. This enables the angler to more effectively fish a piece of structure or other desired fish-holding areas.

MAPPING AND CARTOGRAPHY

The contour and bottom mapping capabilities of sonar and fishing-finders can add and new set of dimensions to the smart angler's fishing toolkit. The ability to either download maps or create one's own set of charts is a way of notating areas that have produced fish in the past or are worthy of future exploration. New units can present bottom, contours, and structure in exquisite detail and in a multi-dimensional format. Downloadable software in the form of digital map cards can even provide mapping detail that highlights an entire spectrum of water conditions that are of interest to an angler, like depth profiles, contour lines, and even a view from above that results from digitized aerial photography. This feature can give the angler the ability to view and access many geographical and topographic elements like boulders, rock piles, creeks, channels, vegetation and weed lines, sand bars, reefs, mud flats, and drop-offs. Obviously, this sort of "view" can aid immensely in determining the location of fish. In many respects this unique feature shows that the sky is the limit in modern electronics for the angler.

VERTICAL IMAGING

Most manufacturers of fish finders have product offerings that access what is occurring immediately beneath the hull of the boat. The Humminbird company refers to their trademarked technology as Down Imaging, while Lowrance calls it Down Scan Imaging, and Garmin calls it Down VU. Regardless of the designation, this form of technology enables the fish-finding device to project detailed images of the area beneath the boat. These images would include the bottom, as well as any structures and any fish life that exist between the transducer/keel and immediate bottom. The pictures are basically the result of return sonar signals that paint a realistic "digital" representation of what lies beneath the boat.

SIDE SCAN SONAR IMAGING

This form of imaging system utilizes a transducer that broadcasts conical signals downward and across the broad expanse of water off to the sides of the boat. In essence, side scan give the angler a port and starboard view. In most applications it results in detailed representation of a lake bottom or sea floor. The obvious benefit to the angler is the opportunity to visualize what is taking place on a horizontal plane beneath the boat. When combined with vertical imaging the end result is a comprehensive rendition of what is not only directly beneath the boat but on the periphery as well. As we will see in the next paragraph, further application of CHIRP technology will add yet another dimension to the angler's view with greater clarity of detail and accuracy.

CHIRP

The acronym CHIRP stands for Compressed High Impact Radar Pulse. Although this technology has been around for many decades, it is gaining popularity for its effectiveness as a fish-finding tool. This feature is available on many of today's modern fish finders. What differentiates CHIRP from standard sonar systems it that unlike basic sonar's transmission of one signal at a time, CHIRP transmits a series of multiple signals. This results in more information that produces better image quality, higher resolution, and less signal distortion. The net effect of all this is that the smart angler can more easily interpret the signal representations that appear on the screen. For instance, an angler using CHIRP can better differentiate between feeding fish and bait and, with some experience interpreting signals, the types and size of targeted fish species. The clarity of the images also gives a more intuitive understanding of what you see on-screen.

DIGITAL FISHING EXPLORATION AND ONLINE SOCIAL NETWORKS

The modern, smart angler has more at his or her disposal than the electronic hardware and software described previously in this chapter. In many respects, "the world is your oyster" with regard to information that is relevant and instantly available. Much of that opportunity has to do with the Internet, specialized software applications, and the phenomenon that is social media. Never has there been a time in history where access to data has been so instantaneous. Press a few keys on your computer, phone, or mobile device, and presto, you enter another dimension of time and space. This form of access has had very meaningful impact upon all segments of society, including the world of fishing. Two striking examples of this are Google Earth and Google Maps. In the good old days one would have to pore over nautical maps or make exploratory runs to areas to get a feel for the underwater topography and how it might affect the fishing. Now, you can accomplish that and much more while sitting at home in your favorite recliner. If you are interested in fishing a new body of water you can access it via Google Earth or Google Maps and then take a virtual tour of the destination. Be it lake, stream, ocean or bay, your digital explorations can yield valuable fishing insights. You can achieve aerial views and the ability to zoom in on prominent structural features of a particular body of water without ever having to splash one's boat in the water. In the final analysis, this can save the angler a lot of wasted time when it comes to actually fishing that location. Having advance knowledge of the topography of a body of water also enables an angler to develop an advance plan to fishing that location. While nothing can ever replace the value of on-water experience, digital tours of the fishing grounds can indeed cut the learning curve. I have fished an area of the Long Island Sound for more than four decades and have a reasonably intimate understanding of bottom structure and other bait and fish-attracting features. Years on the water, studying maps, and running my own fish finders over those areas have given me a good idea of that specific underwater world. Yet it wasn't until I decided to take a virtual tour of that area and get a bird's eye view did I realize how much I had been missing. Much to my amazement I got to see an array of features that I never knew existed, features that eventually led me to more fish.

In addition to the specific Google applications referenced there are many other websites, "apps," and social media forums where anglers can increase their own fishing IQ. In-depth information is out there for the taking on just about any fishing-related subject: fish species, bait, fishing techniques, equipment, lures, boats, knots, electronics, and destinations. All one need do is organize their searches to cast as wide or as narrow a net to retrieve the necessary information. Just a simple online search of fishing applications will produce a plethora of unique software. One cautionary note regarding those websites that post general fishing reports: If you have spent any considerable time on the water you fully realize that fish reported in one area one day may very well be gone the next day. Unless fish are fully entrenched in an area, chasing online fishing reports can prove futile. I don't know any excellent anglers who hotly pursue specific reports other than to understand if fish are in a general area. While online fishing reports are certainly timelier than are printed accounts in hard copy publications, the critical element in finding fish is to go where they are expected to be, rather than where they have been. Plus, one has to contend with the potential for social media hyperbole. I once read of an angler having an "epic" day, only to discover that in his relative view of the world the grand day involved catching three fish. While every catch is meaningful in its own way, I would not normally characterize a three-fish day as being epic, unless of course they were exceptional specimens or caught in a unique and challenging way. That said, online or stale reports in other forms of media should be taken with a grain of salt. In my book, it is always much better to make your own "reports" by finding your own fish. I will add that some of the social media discussion boards and chat rooms that deal with fishing can prove quite useful in helping to promote an exchange of ideas and information. And many of the better forums can prove to be educational and help the angler cut down on the learning curve. Choose your participation wisely and you will reap the benefits. Some of the more popular and useful applications, especially for mobile devices, are Fishidy, Fishbrain, Pro Angler, First Mate, Knot Guide, Go Free Hooked, and Navionics. These can either be general in nature or quite specific to the targeted needs of anglers.

Captain John Raguso of MarCeeJay Sportfishing Charters is an acknowledged offshore fishing expert who enjoys consistent success off the south shore of Long Island. Captain John is also a prolific writer who has written countless reviews of boats, marine electronics, and other related gear. His perspectives and advice on marine electronics is especially relevant to this discussion, particularly as they pertain to the application and management of those electronics. Captain John believes in the Noah's Ark Principle of Marine Electronics Management: Take Two of Everything. Here's John's wisdom gleaned from decades of time on the water:

Having been an offshore boater/angler/mate since the mid 1970s and a charter boat captain since the late 1980s, I have logged over a thousand offshore trips and have seen and done just about everything. When it comes to marine electronics, I am a firm believer in the Noah's Ark principle of marine electronics management and literally take two of everything onboard. My current MarCeeJay (#14) is an unsinkable 2006 Edgewater 228cc that went through a complete marine electronics transformation after I bought her back in November of 2014. Since her mission is to be equally capable finding tuna forty miles offshore as she is plying the inshore waters of the Peconics and Shinnecock Bay, I removed all of the old electronics and updated this center console with a pair of Furuno GP1870F combo GPS Chartplotter/Echo Sounders with 7-inch diagonal screens. I chose the Furunos since they have legendary commercial-grade quality, were made in Italy with European craftsmanship, and featured clear/bright color screens that didn't wash out when wearing polarized sunglasses.

Each unit includes a built-in GPS antenna, so by mounting two of these machines side-by-side, I have them set up as with one as a dedicated GPS/navigator and the other a standalone fish finder. If one machine has a hiccup, the other can be tasked to perform both functions in an emergency, albeit with all of the critical info crammed into a single 7-inch screen. I also installed two transducers, with one on the transom and the other glued in the hull in "shoot-thru" mode. Taking the two-of-everything approach even further with my marine electronics, I have two VHF antennas installed, with a fixed-mount VHF radio and a battery-powered handheld as a back-up. I also have two sea temperature gauges, which are critical for detecting sea surface temperature breaks offshore. One is a dedicated Si-Tex ST-110 with a large LED display and the other is on the Furuno's quadducer and shows a reading on one of the GP1870's data screens. Taking this two-of-everything approach even further, I also carry a hand-held (battery-powered) GPS just in case my twin 27-series marine batteries ever quit. And in case you wondered,

Captain John Raguso believes in the principle of redundancy with regard to his fishing and safety-related electronics. CREDIT: JOHN RAGUSO

yes, I also have two engines on my boat, a Yamaha F225 four-stroke as primary power, supported by a Mercury 9.9-hp four stroke as a get-home kicker. The Noah's Ark marine management process works for me.

CHAPTER 17

SELECTED TIPS, TACTICS, AND TECHNIQUES

As with any athletic endeavor or sport, there's no substitute for practice and real-time experience. And so it is with fishing. The simple fact is the more time you spend on the water the more capable you will become at dealing with the various factors that lead to success. Whether your measure of accomplishment is many fish per outing, trophy fish, or catching specific species in the manner in which you choose, nothing provides you with the finely-tuned skills necessary for consistent fishing more than your own self-education. Books like this one can give you a solid foundation for getting into the game. Videos, websites, and social media can help answer some of your most basic questions. But nothing replaces the lessons you learn from the fish you find and catch, or from the ones you don't catch. When I give presentations to clubs or other organizations, I often say that the bad fishing outings often teach us more than the good ones, and that fishing is a recreation, sport, or profession that requires continual learning and continual improvement. One need only keep an open mind and maintain a willingness to improve. Never has that been more evident than in today's angling world, with the abundance of artificial baits at an angler's disposal. Along with very specialized modern tackle, we have seen the arrival of smart baits that can challenge the angler to think more precisely about suitable applications. What this means is that the "one size fits all" mentality may no longer fit the bill when one fishes. It is the thinking angler who has the greatest success. This is the angler who comprehends all aspects of his or her sport and seeks to understand more than just the basics. We see specialization at work in all aspects of fishing. And while we have addressed that in previous chapters, it is worth repeating that the modern angler is challenged with decisions each and every time he or she steps in a boat or sets foot in the water. Once a day's fishing strategy is in place for a particular body of water, one's choice of tackles and gear becomes the next significant decision.

When fishing from a boat it pays to follow the lead of freshwater bass anglers. They carry an array of rods rigged with baits to meet most of the conditions or scenarios that they will reasonably encounter. Rather than having to constantly change baits, the rods are at the ready for immediate use, should the situation arise. When wade or bank fishing is the game, a backpack or fanny pack is ideal for organizing or storing baits and other items essential to a successful outing. Should surf fishing be your cup of tea, then a quality surf bag will suffice. Fly anglers can choose storage systems that range between pocketed and compartmentalized vests, chest packs, shoulder packs, or hip packs. With the variety of artificial smart baits currently at the disposal of anglers, choosing a set of possible baits can be an overwhelming experience, especially to the novice angler. A few general rules can make this process a bit less daunting. First and foremost, and depending on the targeted species, the specific fishing conditions and the type of available bait, it is a good idea to always choose your highest-confidence artificial

Smart baits come in all shapes, sizes, and colors.

as a first choice. Simply put, that is the bait in which you place the most trust and the bait that has yielded the best results over time. Whether that artificial is a topwater plug, crank bait, diving plug, darter, stick bait, soft plastic, or suspending bait, go with it as the primary choice. If the lure produces, great. If not, move on to another set of suitable choices. A practical approach is to make sure that you have an assortment of smart baits to prospect all levels of the water column as well as structure and cover. Select baits that appeal to all aspects of a fish's feeding habits, predatory behaviors, sensory, and reactive instincts, as well as the prevalent bait.

We discussed the importance of retrieves in a previous chapter and that aspect of the game cannot be understated. One of the risks of having so many modern smart bait choices is that some anglers get conditioned to constant lure changing. Time and again I have seen that it is always better to vary the retrieve before changing lures. Take for instance a topwater chugging plug that spits, spurts, and pops. Many years ago while fishing the surf for striped bass I experienced a retrieving lesson that has stood the test of time. I was fishing a boulder field during the beginning of an outgoing tidal flow. The topwater plug that I was using made a lot of noise and pushed a ton of water. It was a bait that replicated the splashing of Atlantic menhaden, a favorite food choice of stripers. But as the old saying goes, "no one was home." Or at least that is what appeared to be the situation. The particular spot I was fishing often had a productive window of opportunity of about forty-five minutes to an hour, tops. I was about halfway through that period and had not a single strike to show for my efforts. I was about to change lures, thinking that would change my luck. But then during one of the retrieves I abruptly stopped popping the plug and gathering line to re-adjust the surf bag that had slid uncomfortably off my shoulder. After I tightened the shoulder strap, I began to impart some life back into the plug that had remained motionless in the water. No sooner had the plug started to move when a bass smacked it with its tail and returned to grab the easy pickings. Over the years I have become in-tune with subtle signs and signals that fish reveal, so I made another cast. But this time at a point about half way into the retrieve I stopped the plug and let it rest on the surface of the water for what must have been about thirty seconds. I then twitched the rod tip and "whammo," another bass hit the plug. That changeup to the retrieve proved to be the pattern for the day's fishing. Once the bite ended and I made way back to my truck I stored that lesson for future use and added that tactic to my medley of retrieves. It has since proven to be a game-changer for me. There are many examples like that one that can guide an angler before changing lures. Here's one more case in point that illustrates how retrieve and color can make a difference when using modern smart baits.

Little tunny, also known as false albacore or albies, are often a challenging species for inshore fly and light-tackle anglers. A friend and I had encountered a solid number of migratory fall pods of albies that were feeding aggressively. We both fished with a similar modern epoxy bait, but each in a different color. That tactic enabled us to determine if color would be a key factor to success. Angling partners can also fish different lures to achieve much the same end result. But as it turned out for us, the first pod of fish we came upon didn't distinguish between colors and we both hooked fish. After landing a number of albies it appeared that the fish became a bit more selective and would only strike the white bait, totally ignoring the pink version. And then the fish rotated back to pink and subsequently amber. The reason for this behavior eventually became quite evident. The fish were moving between rafts of different species of baitfish, each of which showed highlights of varied tones, colors, and hues. On this day color did indeed make a difference. But our education didn't stop there.

At one point during the morning, the bite completely shut down. No matter what colors we tried we could not get another fish. As we approached one pod of false albacore my partner made a long cast beyond and ahead of the feeding fish. He quickly gathered line to get his lure into the strike zone and held the rod tip exceedingly high while reeling. The lure moved rapidly and skimmed across the surface. The lure's path eventually intersected with the direction that the fish were travelling. And then bingo! Fish on! We both immediately realized what had happened. We needed to skim the lure across the surface of the water. For the rest of the bite it mattered not what color lure we used as long as the jig was kept in motion atop the water. At the time, it appeared to us that the motion of the lure generated by that very specific retrieve mimicked the way in which the baitfish were leaping from the water to escape their pursuers. But whatever the reason, once we determined cause and effect, the fish responded with continual reaction strikes.

When all was said and done, we caught albies for two complete tide cycles. Although this experience involved the use of an epoxy jig and a saltwater game fish the same thought process applies to any other artificial bait and any other species of fish. Even those anglers engaged in offshore

Space age epoxies have made jigging lure more versatile and more effective.

trolling vary the speed of their troll, alter the trolling distance behind the boat, and use different color and size lures in their spread. They also rig baits to swim differently when trolled. For example, some baits might swim just below the surface of the water, whereas others create topwater commotion while skipping along the top. That variation of technique will appeal to the different striking moods that fish may be in, and may help to establish a pattern for that specific day's bite.

Although contemporary smart baits are engineered to swim with out-of-the-box precision, many seasoned anglers are inclined to modify their baits to matching certain fishing conditions. For example, surf casters are well known for "loading" their swimming plugs to achieve greater casting distance and enhanced swimming action. Loading entails adding additional weight to the plug in the form of a liquid, most often water. A small hole pierced into the plastic allows you to add liquid to the desired level. Some trial-and-error field testing is required to get the weight and balance right so that the lure swims well. Anglers also tune their baits to change the way they react when retrieved, and to achieve an optimal swimming motion. This modification usually comes in the form of adjustment to the lip or bill of a bait. Freshwater anglers, especially those who fish the professional circuit, are very much proponents of lure tuning. It bears repeating that even the most sophisticated smart baits, both hard and soft baits, might very well benefit from tuning. That could take the form of loading plugs as described above or something relatively simple as changing hooks to either achieve a different swim pattern or for ease of removal. Other types of custom changes that anglers make include modifications like inserting weights or BBs to alter a lure's balance, adding rattles or beads to create more sound, sanding down the lips on swimming plugs, adding customized paint jobs to a lure, and using a variety of trailer add-ons for greater lure movement and appeal. When it comes to variations of this type, anglers are limited only by their imaginations and creativity. If there is a scenario that requires changing a bait's basic construction, then have at it. Tools and materials are readily available to the "crafty" angler, and most often many of those items are obtainable at a local craft store.

While making changes to modern production lures is a fairly common practice among smart anglers, there is yet another group that has totally taken matters into their own hands. These anglers are also active lure designers who custom build their artificials to their own needs and specifications. Whether fabricated from wood, plastic, or metal this aspect of the sport is much akin to how fly tiers design and tie personalized fly patterns. And many of these designers are incorporating an array of smart features into their baits, with creativity being the only limitation. One need not be a highly-skilled craftsman to transform a simple bait into a more productive lure with added "smart" traits. An ordinary plastic worm or other soft plastic bait can serve as a vivid example of such adaptation. You could cut open the head of a plastic bait and hollow out a small space for beads or rattles, then glue the cut closed. In similar fashion, you could place weight at any point in the bait to change its balance and the way it swims. Using indelible ink markers, you could add unique color patterns to better reflect the baitfish in the area or to give the bait more appeal. That same plastic bait could then be enhanced further with the application of scent. So with a few minor adaptations, you can make over a quite ordinary plastic bait and convert it into a smart lure that can tempt multiple senses of targeted fish species. With some imagination and creativity, any form of artificial lure can undergo uncomplicated yet effective changes.

CHAPTER 18

THE SMARTEST BAIT IS YOU

There is no doubt that today's recreational anglers have at their disposal the most modern and high-tech artificial baits ever presented to game fish. As we have already seen those same anglers also have access to rods, reels, and lines that are wonders of modern technology. But tools are only as good as the craftsman or craftswoman who uses them. In the hands of a less-than-competent practitioner, even the most sophisticated tools will most likely yield less than ideal results. So it is with fishing. While quality gear helps all levels of angler proficiency, it is the smart angler who maximizes the potential of his or her equipment. In many respects the informed, inquisitive, and intellectual angler is, in essence, the smartest bait of all. Learning as much as you can from each and every outing is imperative to improved angling results and consistent success. I experienced a situation a number of years ago that put into perspective for me many of the principles that have led me down a path of continual learning and continual improvement regarding my own fishing. While this event involved a fly-fishing outing, its lessons were far-reaching and affected how I also pursued all other forms of fishing. The following anecdote illustrates the principles that can help anyone become a better angler.

The approaching thunderstorm was still a long distance off, but it was definitely moving in my direction. The turbulence was laced with healthy doses of lightning and that would not bode well for wading a stretch of isolated beach with a nine-foot lightning rod in hand. Checking the weather application on the phone, the radar indicated that there were about forty-five minutes left to fish before things would get nasty. The low-pressure system had already been kind, offering up two striped bass willing to eat flies. One fish was 26 pounds, the other 27½ pounds. As things turned out, my remaining time on the beach would yield one more nice surprise. But time was not an ally, and there was only one fifty-yard section of the beach remaining that could reasonably produce fish given the current conditions. The tide phase was perfect for that location and the current formations would be ideal with the building wind. Hoofing it there posthaste, I went to a small sand bar that jutted out from the beach and intersected a trough within casting distance. In past outings, success here has come swinging flies in the current that formed off the tip of the sand bar. Conditions for that were perfect and it didn't take long for one hefty jolt to validate the presence of fish; it was another good bass. The quality of that striper was confirmed 15-minutes later when I lipped a bass slightly over thirty pounds. As I released the fish to rejoin the others that had been set free earlier, the thunder and rain was upon me. I felt a bit like the priest in the movie *Caddyshack*, who had just played the best golf game of his life only to be struck by a bolt from the heavens. Not wanting my day to end that way, I expeditiously made my way, back to the truck.

Subsequently thinking about that outing it became very apparent that connecting the dots on the water was the key to salvaging what could have been an otherwise dismal morning. Figuring out a changing "puzzle" is always the means for achieving consistent results when fishing. The best anglers I know are skilled in many aspects of fishing and are capable of adapting equipment,

Connecting the dots when fishing, and solving the ever-changing puzzles that the fish present, are the true keys to success.

tactics and techniques to a wide range of fishing scenarios. They fully comprehend the general dynamics of fishing and use all tools at their disposal in an appropriate manner. Those folks also have, first and foremost, an intimate understanding of the relationship between bait and game fish. Recognizing the behaviors and migratory patterns of both prey and predator is essential to consistent success on the water. Over the years I have had countless experiences that have broadened my understanding and appreciation of surf environments. And I've also learned much from the experiences of others. The principles and practices that follow have served me and other fly anglers well on the beach. Perhaps they might offer you some insight into your own brand of fishing. These principles can apply whether you fish in freshwater or saltwater, and regardless of the species pursued.

1.   **Learn to read water and gain a thorough understanding of the environment within the surf zone, especially the behavioral patterns and interactions of predators and prey.** Also try to visualize what is going on beneath the surface of the water, especially with regard to structure and the resulting movements of water and bait. Many anglers sometimes simply approach a fishing spot and begin casting without so much as taking time to assess the surroundings, or what is occurring on or beneath the surface. Whether on a boat in the ocean or wading a small trout stream, take a moment to stop, look, and listen, while embracing the environment. I once fished a beach at the break of dawn to find just a solitary gull there to join me. Although I started to walk in one direction along the beach, the bird flew in the opposite direction. By its demeanor and attitude I decided to change my path and follow the bird. Within minutes, false albacore began breaking the surface close enough to the beach for me to get in some productive casts with the fly rod. The gull knew more than I did, and even though there was no apparent surface activity at the time it sensed what was happening underwater. Paying attention to nature's signals that morning proved rewarding.

2.   **Understand and recognize fish-attracting structure and spend time determining how best to fish those configurations.** This principle is equally important whether your fishing takes you to a freshwater bass lake, a river, or a jetty that juts out into the open ocean. When it comes to structure, a broadened definition that embraces both natural and man-made forms is also the most appropriate. Be aware of anything out

of the ordinary along at your chosen fishing hole. As an example: even a slight bend or depression in a shoreline could be enough of a structure break to affect your fishing outcome. Some of the more classic forms of fish-attracting and holding areas include boulder fields, channels, cuts, docks, sunken timber, piers, sunken barges, boats and rock piles. One of my most productive fishing beach spots is an area that holds a bunch of large concrete blocks that fell from a construction barge in the 1930s. Hardly anyone knows they are there, except for the town historian. Take your fishing wisdom from any and all sources.

3.   **One of the keys to becoming an exceptional angler is the desire to explore.** There will surely be times when you arrive at your destination to find fish on the move, but those situations are often exceptions, not the rule. Hiking, boating, biking, kayaking, canoeing, or driving to get to productive areas often works much better than standing in one spot while waiting for fish to turn on. And when you venture forth to an unfamiliar stretch of water, you just might discover your own slice of productive water. But that "walkabout" is not just a serendipitous stroll in the park. The watchful and alert angler is the one who most often bags the most fish. Successful anglers plan each outing and where they will fish, rather than leave the day's results to happenstance. There are many factors that go into preparing a day's fishing plan, and most of those elements come with experience and acquired knowledge from time on the water, as well as making your own discoveries.

4.   **Adapt your fishing strategies and tactics to best match the uniqueness of each form of fishing scenario.** Some of the situations that you will encounter include: Sand and cobble beaches, inlets, jetties, flats, harbors, bays, back country, river mouths, tidal creeks, points, coves, vegetation, islands, and salt ponds. Each circumstance presents its own challenges and opportunities. For example, during the early spring and then again during the fall run, sand beaches that attract sand eels and/or white bait will often be the most productive places to fish. Likewise, a favorite wading flat might light up during that transition period between spring and summer. Jetties and inlets might be the ticket to some great late summer fishing when pelagic visitors like Atlantic bonito and little tunny make their way north. And fish like striped bass will still venture onto summer flats in many bays along with the cooler

water of an incoming tide. In freshwater, early season bass hot spots will include coves that warm first. And in the fall, docks and rock points might do the trick.

5. **Learn from the land that is adjacent to the water.** The gradient of land masses often holds clues to how land slopes once it meets and merges with water. On more than one occasion following sloping terrain has led to a hole or depression that either holds or attracts bait fish, often well within reach of an angler's cast. The best time to explore the potential of an area and get the "lay of the land" is during extreme low tide or water conditions. Prey and predator proximity to shore is especially relevant when fishing shallow, since those conditions put game fish well within a shore caster's reach. In many regions of the country, both spring and fall months will see quarry moving to and from these zones. These can be high-activity and high-productivity periods for the angler, and often it is a sloping drop-off or troughs that will attract fish.

6. **Time of day is another important consideration, and it is also tied to seasons.** The general rule of fishing the false dawn period to an hour or so after sunrise and then again the magic time around dusk and sunset is a good one to follow. The period from about 11 p.m. to 2 a.m. is another great time slot, especially for nocturnal feeding species. Never neglect to fish during the day if your schedule allows. This is especially relevant during the early spring and the fall run. Even high noon can be a great time for spotting and catching migrating fish on sand or mud flats, or in the water that touches the shoreline.

7. **Hydrodynamics is one of the most important factors for consistent fishing success.** The interrelationship of tides, currents, still water, and moving water is also important, especially between tides and currents. In many respects those two factors are mutually dependent. Tidal movements and currents are two of your best allies when fly fishing the surf. Currents are influenced by many factors, including: intensity of tides; contour of the coast line; surface and sub-surface structure like jetties, rock formations and underwater boulders; channels; troughs; areas where water funnels and accelerates; and water temperature and wind. Both forms of water flow influence movements and feeding behaviors of bait and game fish. Fish will transition deeper into inter-tidal areas on the flood and follow bait with retreating water.

For example, striped bass will often move on and off flats with flooding and ebbing tides. Fish will also feed deeper into marshes, along grass lines, in harbors and back country areas on high water, and again move out with falling water. Predatory fish naturally gravitate toward areas of current where they can ambush bait as it is flushed out to them. Still water presents its own challenges as does moving water of rivers, streams, and creeks. Spending time learning all one can about the local waters that you fish will yield substantial dividends in the form of more successful outings.

8. **Practice.** Just like professional baseball players continually practice their hitting, so it is with successful anglers who continually practice their casting. Good anglers become proficient in all forms of fishing tackle, be it spinning, casting, or fly, and with all varieties of artificial baits. Learn to cast well and practice regularly. Distance in some instances is important but accuracy of the cast is always most important. And experiment with retrieves. Not all artificial baits work to their fullest potential with the application of just one form of retrieve. Accurate casts, coupled with varied and suitable retrieves will always produce more strikes. Given that fishing conditions vary, practice casting from a number of different positions and attitudes. Fish don't always come at you head-on, so learn to cast laterally, sidearm, and backhanded. I know anglers who practice casting on one foot, kneeling down, in the water, on rocks, etc. It is kind of like a baseball player practicing to pull the ball, go to the opposite field, or bunt. Be prepared for what the fish or the weather throws at you. There are times when I am on the water during slow periods of fishing and I entertain myself by casting to a variety of floating objects and targets. It is important to always keep that casting edge honed.

9. **Seasons.** No matter where one fishes, the spring and fall months are typically prime-time periods. Most game fish, whether freshwater or saltwater, will exhibit heightened activity at these times. That can be as a result of pre- or post-spawning activity, the abundance of bait-fish at those times of year, or ideal water conditions. The hotter summer months can either be boom or bust depending on where the fishing occurs, and the time of day one fishes. During fall months, especially in the colder regions, anglers will experience the most

intensely-concentrated fishing of the year as fish put on the feed bag and migrate. And certainly, winter fishing in the southeast and throughout the gulf coast can be spectacular.

10. **The moon and the wind.** Much has been written about the best moon phases for fishing. In the final analysis, new moon and full moon phases both have their advocates. Some anglers will fish religiously for two or three days on either side of a new moon, while others will totally ignore the new moon and concentrate all their efforts around the big tides of a full moon, and to use winds to your advantage. Anglers often view wind as the number one nemesis of many anglers, but it can be an ally. Winds coming off the water and onto the beach will often push baitfish into the surf zone where predatory fish will follow. While extreme winds certainly present challenging and often overwhelming casting conditions, moderate wind can be an angler's friend. And don't shy away from using the fly rod on blustery days. Learn how to cast into a stiff breeze and you will reap fly-fishing benefits many others miss. Practice and intentionally use a fly rod in adverse conditions. My best fly rod day ever was in Alaska catching bright coho salmon nonstop between 40 mph gusts with sustained winds over 20 mph. The same scenario can play out along the surf. I've experienced that, too with success. In some of those instances bass were right up along the edge of the beach, where short casts got the job done.

11. **Tactical fishing.** Some anglers prefer to stay put in one known productive spot while others are constantly on the move, opting to seek fish out rather than wait for them to come to them. That approach is not one of aimlessly walking about but rather part of a strategy that embraces many of the elements previously discussed: season and time of day, tide phase, current flow, and bait movements. How, where, and when one fishes is determined through assimilation of that knowledge and projecting where the bite is most likely to occur. Play the tides, play the winds, and above all else, if your exploring brings you to masses of baitfish, fish that area thoroughly. This tactic is valid whether one wades, or fishes from a boat or other conveyance. Have a plan at the start of your fishing day and think through your fishing strategy. And always have a Plan B and a Plan C, since nature, fish, weather, and the environment have a habit of throwing some mean curve balls.

12.   **Be prepared.** Bad things can happen quickly on and around water, even on the calmest of small ponds. Pay attention to the surroundings. Shifting sands from storms can create new hazards and jetties can be especially dangerous. Wade cautiously and rather than plodding ahead while wading, take it slow. Shuffle your feet laterally as you move, instead of taking big blind steps. This helps prevent unexpected falls from deeper pockets of water. Water hazards are everywhere for the boating angler and a calm ride to the fishing grounds can be a nightmare on the return trip if winds and waves become unfriendly. Additionally, there is nothing more frustrating than being on the water or on a beach or on some expansive sand flat only to realize you left a critical piece of angling gear back in your vehicle, or at home. If you plan on spending an entire day on the water, pack some extra gear and essentials in a backpack or fanny pack. And if need be, bring a lunch, snack, and something to drink. You don't want hunger or thirst to hamper your efforts when the fishing turns on. And always have a means for communicating with emergency help if that situation arises. If you carry a cell phone or a hand held VHF, make sure it is readily accessible and protected. While most contemporary emergency gear of this nature are waterproof, it doesn't hurt to keep those devices secure in waterproof bags.

Those of us who love to fish are very fortunate to live during a time when technological innovation reigns supreme. Our equipment and baits have been a beneficiary of those scientific advancements. Artificial lures are smarter, tackle is smarter, electronics are smarter. But the angler needs to be the smartest factor in the equation. Keep learning, keep asking why, explore and experiment, and just go out and have some fun.

CHAPTER 19

ARTI-FISH-IAL INTELLIGENCE: WHERE DO WE GO FROM HERE?

In 1961 author Jim Westman published a book titled, *Why Fish Bite and Why They Don't*. It was a unique treatise on angling and the first book that I had read which discussed the science of fish behavior. In particular, the focus of the volume was on specific behaviors and angling methods that motivate fish to strike a bait. At the time I read this book, I was in my early teens and had visions of becoming a famous marine biologist, so the three chapters that intrigued me most were: The Art and Science of Fishing; The Art and Science in Freshwater; and The Art and Science in Saltwater. To a young angler with an interest in fish biology, I was riveted to the words on those pages. In my brief angling experiences, those chapters represented for me the first time that fishing was framed in concepts other than the choice of equipment, casting technique, how to select a bait or lure, or any other technical aspect of sport fishing. Those sixty-two pages represented an entirely new perspective on the relationship between science and fishing, and changed my outlook entirely on fishing and my personal fishing methods.

It was not until 1973 and a book written by Mark Sosin and John Clark, titled *Through the Fish's Eye*, that I was once again captivated by very special insights into the behaviors of fish. But in this book the authors take the reader on a tour of the anatomic senses of fish and how that physiology affects general behavior, feeding patterns, and the selection of food. I readily consumed this information and when applied to real world fishing situations, I ultimately elevated my own angling game. I fast became an ardent disciple of linking science to fishing. And to this day, all of my fishing, regardless of the method or species pursued, involves the discipline of trying to "think" like a fish. Obviously, fish don't think in human terms, but we know well that they do respond and react to various stimuli and prompts which include their environment, their senses, and their instincts. This applies to the way in which fish respond to artificial lures, especially modern smart baits. As we have seen in the previous chapters, modern baits represent a totally new level of sophistication in both design and application. Modern bait engineering fully embraces the principles of science, fish biology, and fish sensory mechanisms. Some might suggest that we have reached the peak of design effectiveness of artificial lures, but that is not the way of ingenuity and design. Those who designed and drove the first "horseless carriage" would be enthralled by the engineering marvels that are modern automobiles. Both Alexander Graham Bell and Thomas Edison would be thrilled by the invention of the cell phone and the concept of transmitting wireless messages. All modern technological and scientific advances that human society enjoys stand upon the creativity of previous generations. And so it is with the art and science of fishing and the creation of advanced lures.

As part of the process of writing this book I have spoken with many lure designers, manufacturers, anglers, and fishing industry research and development folks on the subject of how smart baits will evolve. It appears that the long view for next-generation artificial baits goes something like this. We will see much more focus on realistic movement of baits. Articulation and segmentation are growing in popularity in all forms of artificial baits: hard

The time-tested Al's Goldfish has a new look that embraces many of the principles of smart lure design.

baits, soft baits, flies, bucktails, and jigs. With practiced retrieves, these baits truly do look alive in the water so the future should see much more refinement of movement. Some also expect to see the continued offering of bigger baits and more realistic shapes and profiles. It has been an oft-repeated mantra of the fishing world that "big fish eat big baits." Anglers have proved that proposition time and again with the advent of modern smart baits. The principle has been tested successfully in freshwater and saltwater, and there is an expectation that larger baits will trend well into the future. Enhanced sound will also become more prevalent in artificial baits. There are many success stories and anecdotes surrounding the use of sound such as rattles and bead and pulsating digital signals. But where this may all lead to is the creation of sounds that are unique signatures of specific prey baits that predatory fish relate to. For example, the splashing noises made by surface-romping menhaden or mullet may in the future be replicated for their frequency and tonal qualities which more realistically reflect the sounds transmitted by those fish. And in the cast of those two baits, striped bass or tarpon many be more keyed to those sounds than other vibrations. Replicating those distinctive sounds within artificial baits could very well make them much more targeted when attracting game fish and, therefore, generate more strikes.

Scent too will continue to be a critical element with new-age baits, particularly with soft baits. There will be more of a trend toward infused scents, but anglers will continue to use stick applicators for hard plastic baits

Popping plugs are very effective for targeting a fish's sense of sound.

and metals. The expectation is that scent will also become more targeted with regard to mimicking specific natural baits, and manufactured with a chemistry that generates a physiological response from predatory fish. New high-tech materials will become integral parts of future baits to enhance durability. This has significance for two reasons: Anglers are targeting bigger and more powerful fish with lighter and stronger tackle, and given the price of some of today's baits, anglers don't want throw-away lures after only a couple of fish. As science yields better synthetics, resins, and polymers, the lure-making industry will embrace those products to create more resilient and longer-lasting artificial baits.

Color has always been a hotly-debated attribute of artificial lures. Some of the color biases are based in one's confidence in a particular tone or shade, while other beliefs are well-rooted in the principles of how light penetration affects color changes within the water column, and how fish use their sense of vision to find prey. Some anglers get so fixated on specific colors, tones, and shadings that they rarely vary their choice. But the fact remains that color does matter. We are witnessing an era where lure manufacturers are reproducing the color patterns of actual prey bait in exquisite detail. This movement should continue as will efforts to find and produce color combinations that represent what a fish actually sees. Continuing on the trend toward realism, the texture and feel of artificial baits will evolve to be more lifelike when fish actually strike a bait. This natural feel will cause a fish to mouth the bait for a longer period of time than a bait that seems foreign. Lastly, the industry will most likely see more of a tendency to weigh-balance

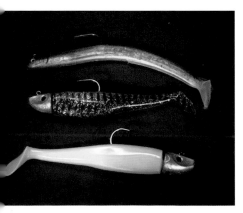

Soft and hard plastic baits are well suited for the application of liquid and stick scents.

Fnhancement with color presentation will continue in an effort to achieve greater realism and more strike-stimulating patterns.

artificial lures to accomplish greater distance when casting and allow the bait to swim in a more natural manner.

All of the items referenced above are possible future enhancements built upon either legacy baits or improvements to contemporary baits. But innovation doesn't have to stop there. The future belongs to those who can think well beyond the modern tackle box, and just like so many other futurists, the designers of future baits have a clean slate that is open to all imaginable possibilities. Some of the world's greatest science fiction writers were Isaac Asimov, H. G.Wells, Ray Bradbury, Jules Verne, George Orwell, Kurt Vonnegut, and Arthur C. Clarke. All had one thing in common: They were visionaries with a superior ability to see a future world that others at the time were unable to comprehend. They shared a rather uncommon space with other genius minds that not only gave us a glimpse into the future but also changed the world in which we live. So too have the likes of Isaac Newton, Alexander Graham Bell, Thomas Edison, Henry Ford, Albert Einstein, Marie Curie, Bill Gates, and Steve Jobs. These pioneers advanced industry, society, science and the human condition. The realm of recreational fishing has piggybacked with many of the advancements made in other industries to improve the products modern anglers use. We've seen that with electronics, plastics, nanofibers, resins, and polymers. Those cutting-edge innovations have affected all segments of the fishing industry: rods, reels, lines, boats, motors, and artificial baits. But the twenty-first century may very well usher in an era of "biomimicry."

According to the Merriam-Webster Dictionary, biomimicry or biomimetics, is "the imitation of natural biological designs or processes in engineering or invention." Furthermore, the Oxford Reference expands that definition to include: "A term used by the American naturalist Janine Benyus in *Biomimicry* (1997) to describe features of plants and animals that maximize efficient interaction with the ecosystem, and to advocate human use of similar design features in dwellings, appliances, and equipment that replicate natural systems." Although the origins of this conceptual thinking can most likely be dated to those ancient ancestors who fabricated wings so they could attempt to fly, the more modern roots of biomimicry date to 1948 and a chance encounter with nature that Swiss engineer, George de Mestral, experienced with his dog while walking the woods. Mestral observed how cockleburs stuck to the coat of his dog, and that simple event ultimately lead to the invention of Velcro. There are many such examples of nature-inspired inventions and innovations. From the relationship between woodpeckers and shock absorbers to humpback whales and wind turbines, the kingdoms of the world's flora and fauna have contributed much to how civilizations have advanced. According to the Biomimicry Institute, a quote attributed to Steve Jobs, co-founder of Apple, sums up the future relationship between nature and human civilizations: "I think the biggest innovations of the twenty-first century will be at the intersection of biology and technology. A new era is beginning." And one of the greatest of all biomimetics examples are the human brain, human intelligence, logic, and the process of thinking, and how that all influenced the entire computer industry. But let's take that one step further with the concept of artificial intelligence.

In its purest form, Artificial Intelligence, or "AI," relates to the ability of machines to imitate the cognitive aptitude of humans. In essence, a state of AI is achieved when a mechanical device, computer or machine, is capable of evaluating its environment, learning from experiences, and solving problems. A robot playing a chess game, an automobile driving itself, a voice-recognition system that responds to prompts, are all examples of man-made devices that replicate behaviors driven by artificial intelligence. As science and technology advance, and robotics become more prominent in our daily lives, AI will play a much greater role in how humans and machines interact, even when it comes to smart baits. As we have seen, the design of modern hard and soft baits has relied heavily on science and new technology to create the most sophisticated baits ever to tempt fish to strike. Those advancements have had a direct impact upon how smart baits stimulate the senses of fish with the object of motivating a feeding or reaction strike.

Visionary lure designers can, indeed, imagine the extremes. Perhaps artificial lures could also be engineered to respond to the natural behaviors of prey or predators? For example, what if a smart lure could "sense" the approach of a predatory fish and react in an evasive way, as would a natural bait, and then retain that "learned" behavior for future application. This could almost be like new automobile technology that detects oncoming or peripheral cars. While the objective of the lure is to catch the pursuing fish, the evasion reaction of the bait could be programmed in a way that would allow that bait to be caught by a more agile predator. Or what if the color of a lure could change with varying levels of light penetration as it descends into the depths? Or perhaps a lure could change colors as would a baitfish engaged by the flight response when evading a predator? Maybe a bait could contain an electronic chip that would periodically emit natural distress sounds, or chemical releases that indicate the presence of a stressed or wounded bait fish? I'd be the last one to ever want to take the fun or enjoyment out of fishing by limiting angler involvement in any way to the art of angling, but the fact remains that much, if not all, the technology needed to accomplish these types of smart bait enhancement exists today. It is quite conceivable that combinations of programmed intelligence and robotics could lead to the engineering and development of artificial smart baits that swim and behave much like the natural baits they are intended to simulate. Add to these enhancements elevated taste and feel sensations to further replicate the real thing, and artificial lures can become a very valuable angling tool. In essence, the combination of impressionism, realism, and new-age technology could put a twenty-first century super smart bait into the hands of anglers.

AFTERWORD

We are indeed fortunate as anglers to live in the age that we do. All aspects of our lives have benefitted from rapid advancements in technology, science, and medicine, and fishing has been no exception, as portrayed throughout this entire book. But along with all the good that technology brings comes a requirement to use those capabilities responsibly. Regardless of the industry or application, the primary purpose of technology is to advance civilization and the human condition. Granted, there are indeed legitimate applications that have at their core negative side effects, like military uses of nuclear fission and fusion, but even those forms of innovation can benefit mankind with secondary purposes. Medicine is a prime example of those "piggy-back" opportunities. But with respect to the fishing community, new-age technology has given recreational anglers such improved tools and knowledge that the challenge of fishing can easily turn into the facile sport of "catching." I sometimes wonder if the contest has gotten somewhat lopsided with the strong advantage going to anglers. It seems at times that fish don't stand a chance when coming up against new-age technology. Those are the scenarios when and where responsible and ethical fishing needs to be at the forefront of an angler's sporting principles. We have seen that behavior embraced by angling communities like BASS, Trout Unlimited, the Bonefish Tarpon Trust, and the Atlantic Salmon Federation. Those organizations are advocates not only for sound fisheries management and conservation practices, but for principled and fair chase angling. Those practices are typical of the sporting philosophy of legendary angler Lee Wulff, who said, "game fish are too valuable to be caught only once." While that phrase was the genesis for catch-and-release practices, Wulff's words can have implications well beyond the act of capturing a fish and then releasing it. Some anglers have modified that approach to also suggest limiting one's catch instead of catching one's limit. And therein lies a significant link between modern fishing technology and the ethics of sport angling.

There was a time in the not-too-distant past of many anglers over the age of forty years or so that considered the mark of a successful outing as a full stringer or a cooler packed to the brim with the day's catch. Fortunately for many enlightened anglers, and for the fish as well, that practice has begun to change. With the tools that are at the disposal of modern fishermen and fisherwomen it has become ever easier to accomplish an end result that involves limit catches. But is that total retention of a limit of fish really necessary? Do limits always have to be filled because regulations allow it? I doubt there are many people who enjoy eating fish or seafood more than I do. It is a very regular and staple part of my diet and I would never begrudge anyone from harvesting fish. While I practice diligent catch and release, especially for species whose stocks are in jeopardy, I do occasionally keep fish for the table. But my personal rule is to only take that which my family and I can consume in one or two meals, and I know many other anglers who have also adopted the same practice. Yet I also know some anglers who still pack their freezers to the gills with limits, ultimately to discard most of those fish due to them being beyond the limits of "freshness." I have no intention of either preaching to the choir or the congregation about the virtues of limited harvest or of catch and release. Suffice to say that the sophistication of modern fishing technology in the wrong hands comes with a substantial risk of wanton waste. So I urge all anglers to exercise sound discretion when harvesting their catch to ensure that all future generations of anglers can enjoy the sport we all care about deeply. We all have an obligation to ensure that the legacy we leave includes healthy and abundant stocks of sport fish.

ACKNOWLEDGEMENTS

As any writer will tell you, the process of taking a book from a concept to a physical end product can often be a lonely and somewhat frustrating task. The writer toils away at the keyboard searching for words and sentences that will eventually bring his or her ideas to life. Sometimes the words flow, but sometimes you hit a wall. Very often, moving on to something else for a bit, like a walk on the beach with your dog or going fishing clears the mind, gets the brain's electrical impulses focused on completing the task at hand, and helps inch the draft toward completion. And sometimes the writer needs a few confidants who act as a sounding board for fleshing out ideas. Over the course of writing many books and articles, I have been fortunate to have had access to scores of wonderfully talented folks whose advice, counsel, quotes, and input have indeed enhanced all of my writings. This specific book project was no exception to that, and I'd like to recognize and thank the following folks and organizations for their assistance and contributions. Without their support this book would never have come to fruition.

Thank you: Dr. David Ross, Peter Cowin, BioEdge Fishing Products, Nick Cicero, John Prochnow, Greg Myerson, World Record Striper Company, Dr. William Muller, Chris Paparo, Fish Guy Photos, Mike Laptew, John Skinner, Eric Fieldstat, Roy Leyva, Jerry Gomber, Tsunami Baits, Gary Abernathy, LIVETARGET Lures, Dr. Scott Bronson, Seaguar, Gerry Benedicto, Captain Adrian Mason, Time Flies Sport Fishing, Captain John Raguso, MarCeeJay Sportfishing, Larry Dahlberg, Bob Daly, Tom Gahan, Eposeidon/Kast King, John Stacey, Brooks Robinson, Cortland Line Company, Jay Cassell, Rick Pope, Temple Fork Outfitters, Cliff Pace, Bailey the Lab, Leo the Cat, Tactical Angler, Alberto Knie, Patrick Sebile, Sebile Lures, Berkley Fishing, Al Gag, Whip It Lures, Mike Lee, Al's Goldfish Lure Company, Northbar Tackle, Larry Welcome , Kadir Akturk, AquaSkinz, John Mazurkiewicz, Shimano, Bob Popovics, Dr. Mike Kenfield, Glenn

Mikkleson, Harvey Cooper, Captain Ian Devlin, Captain John Paduano, Premium Bucktails, Tom Keer, Bob Veverka, Steve Piatt, Bill Elliot, Captain Brian Horsley, Laura Pisano, Dennis Zambrotta, Captain David Blinken, Captain Tom Mikoleski, Nancy Hopping, Walter Koda, Captain Terry Nugent, Michael Rioles, Captain Tom Cornicelli, Captain Rick Zaleski, Captain Sandy Noyes, Steve Thomas, David Legg, Bob Clouser, Captain Gary Dubiel, Captain John Luchka, Bob Lindquist, Kevin Arculeo and Lee Weil. And a special thank you to Mark Sosin for his book, *Through the Fish's Eye: An Anglers Guide to Gamefish*. That volume inspired me to think in terms of how fish respond to the stimuli of their environments.

DISCLAIMER

Fishing, like all other water sports, involves a certain degree of risk. It is highly recommended that you practice the sport in a safe way at all times, exercising appropriate and necessary caution, using your acquired skills, judgment, and common sense is essential when in or around water, especially in areas where there are boulders, jetties, or strong currents. Always exercise caution when operating watercraft, when wading or when handling tackle, gear and hooks. If you are unfamiliar with an area, it is strongly recommended that you utilize the services of a professional guide or captain. And always wear a personal floatation device.

FISH CONSUMPTION ADVISORIES

Various state departments of health and environmental conservation maintain up-to-date health advisories pertaining to fish consumption. Please check with those authorities for the general and most current advisories.